THE MAGIC OF
GINGERBREAD

16 BEAUTIFUL PROJECTS TO MAKE AND EAT

WRITTEN AND PHOTOGRAPHED BY
CATHERINE BEDDALL

PETER PAUPER PRESS, INC.
White Plains, New York

THE MAGIC OF GINGERBREAD

Copyright © 2016 by Catherine Beddall
All rights reserved. No part of this book may be used or reproduced in any manner
whatsoever without written permission from the publisher.
First edition 2016

Published by Peter Pauper Press, Inc.
202 Mamaroneck Avenue
White Plains, New York 10601
USA

Designed by Catherine Beddall

Library of Congress Cataloging-in-Publication Data

Names: Beddall, Catherine, author.
Title: The magic of gingerbread : 16 beautiful projects to make and eat /
   written and photographed by Catherine Beddall.
Description: First edition. | White Plains, New York : Peter Pauper Press,
   Inc., 2016. | Includes bibliographical references.
Identifiers: LCCN 2016003632 | ISBN 9781441319807 (hardcover : alk. paper)
Subjects: LCSH: Gingerbread. | LCGFT: Cookbooks.
Classification: LCC TX771 .B38 2016 | DDC 641.86/54--dc23 LC record available at http://lccn.loc.gov/2016003632

ISBN 978-1-4413-1980-7
Manufactured for Peter Pauper Press, Inc.
Printed in Hong Kong

7 6 5 4 3 2 1

Visit us at www.peterpauper.com

This book is for my three favorite gingerbread people:
Tyler, Annabelle, and Sasha. Thank you for all the
love and light you've given me.

CONTENTS

INTRODUCTION

There's something magical about gingerbread.

I love the entire process of creating a gingerbread house, from the initial stages of design and planning, to the first hint of that delicious aroma that fills the kitchen, to seeing it all coming together as a perfect little dream home. (Who wouldn't want to live in a house made of cookies and candy?)

I wasn't always a gingerbread fanatic. I've spent most of my career as a graphic designer, decorating cakes as a part-time business, and only a few years ago made the switch to a full-time career in the pastry arts. It wasn't until I entered and won a local gingerbread house competition that I became totally, irreversibly hooked on creating these sweet little structures. Working with gingerbread simply makes me happy in a way that no other form of edible art does. Why? I think it's a combination of a few different things. There's my love of baking, of course—I've loved to bake for as long as I can remember. Then there's the architectural element—while I don't profess to be an expert on architecture, I've always loved looking at all kinds of houses, both inside and out, and imagining what it would be like to live in them. I've also always been fascinated with the world of miniatures. To me, there's something magical about creating something in miniature, whether it be a house, or any other kind of structure—it's a chance to design a perfect little snapshot in time, a place where the stresses of daily life don't exist. A home away from home.

Anyone can bake and decorate a gingerbread house. I know it might seem easier to buy one of the prefabricated boxed gingerbread house sets you can find at the grocery store around Christmastime. But if you're willing to invest a little bit of time and patience, the results of your handcrafted gingerbread creation will be so much more satisfying—and actually taste like a sweet, spicy cookie and not a chunk of dusty cardboard. I've included a wide array of projects in this book, ranging from easy to advanced. As well as houses, you'll find many fun designs such as cookie puzzles, a chess set, and even a gingerbread robot. The simpler projects are just as beautiful and impressive as the more elaborate ones, and provide an excellent starting point for practicing the skills you'll need as you move on to more advanced projects. Make sure to take the time to read the instructions and explanations carefully, and you'll soon be on your way to creating some stunning showpieces.

In my many, many hours spent testing gingerbread techniques in my own kitchen, I've learned what methods work best, and amassed tons of tips and tricks to help you create your very own masterpiece. I can't wait to share them with you!

~ Catherine

TOOLS
AND
MATERIALS

With surprisingly few tools and materials, you can create anything from the simplest cookies to the most elaborate gingerbread masterpieces. Over the next few pages, you'll find descriptions of the tools and materials I use, and the decorating supplies needed to complete the projects in this book. You probably have many of them in your home already, and the rest are not difficult to find in cake supply, craft, and kitchen stores.

TOOLS

Here's a list of all the tools and materials you need to create the projects in this book. Please note: this list doesn't include basic baking tools. To make the gingerbread dough, you'll need a stand mixer or a sturdy hand mixer, a couple of mixing bowls, measuring cups and spoons, a sieve, and a rubber spatula.

1. **Cookie Sheet.** Make sure it's completely flat—older cookie sheets tend to warp a bit, and it's important for gingerbread to bake completely flat.

2. **Large rolling pin.** Any type of non-tapered, good quality rolling pin will do.

3. **Cooling rack.** It's even more important that your cooling rack be completely flat, because once the gingerbread cools it hardens very quickly.

4. **Paring knife.** A small, sharp paring knife is the best tool to cut gingerbread shapes.

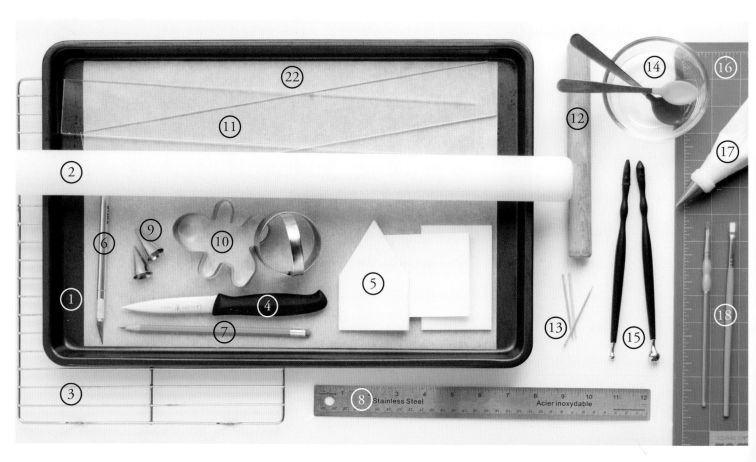

MAKING A TEMPLATE

Templates are essential tools for building any kind of gingerbread structure. They can be cut from a variety of materials; for larger templates, I like to use foam core for its strength and durability, but I've also cut up discarded boxes to create my templates (both corrugated cardboard boxes and lighter ones such as cereal boxes work well). For smaller templates, I recommend using lighter cardboard or thick paper. All of the templates you need for the projects in this book are available in the Templates section at the back of the book.

1.
Photocopy the template outline according to instructions and cut out with scissors.

2.
Place the paper cutout on your template material of choice (I'm using foam core here) and make a dot at each corner with a pencil.

3.
Remove the paper cutout and using a ruler, draw lines joining the dots.

4.
Using a cutting mat, a ruler, and a sharp craft knife, cut out the shape.

5. **Templates.** Templates are shapes cut from any firm material—foam core, cardboard, even thick construction paper—that are used as patterns for gingerbread pieces.

6. **Craft knife.** I use my craft knife to cut templates out of foam core. It's also very handy to cut candies in half as well as small shapes from fondant.

7. **Pencil and eraser.** Used for drawing templates.

8. **Ruler.** Also necessary for drawing templates. (A measurement conversion chart can be found on page 181 for frequently used measurements in the book.)

9. **Piping tips.** Piping tips are placed on the end of a pastry bag to create different piped designs. You'll need a small number of piping tips, mostly varying sizes of round, to create the designs in this book. At the beginning of each project, I'll specify what tips you'll need, and how many.

10. **Cookie cutters.** The cookie cutters you'll need are all readily available online and where cake and cookie decorating supplies are sold. At the beginning of each project, I'll specify what cutters you'll need.

11. **Thickness strips.** I always place two flat strips of plastic on either side of my gingerbread dough when rolling it out, to ensure that it rolls out to an even thickness. Plexiglas sheets of varying thicknesses are available at home stores and can be cut to size. You can roll out gingerbread without these strips, but they are incredibly handy and produce an even sheet of gingerbread every time. Read more about thickness strips on page 24.

12. **Small rolling pin.** I use this for rolling out small pieces of fondant.

13. **Toothpicks.** I use these to add gel food coloring to fondant or royal icing.

14. **Small bowls and spoons.** I use these to mix small amounts of royal icing with food coloring.

15. **Ball tool.** A couple of the projects in this book require a ball tool for shaping fondant. These are readily available at cake decorating supply stores. I recommend getting both a large and medium sized ball tool.

16. **Cutting mat.** Always use one of these when cutting your templates to avoid damaging the surface underneath.

17. **Piping bags and couplers.** You can use either high-quality or plastic disposable piping bags. I recommend having at least 10 piping bags and coupler sets on hand. For most projects, I use a small piping bag.

18. **A few small paintbrushes.** These are used to apply color dusts and for dabbing small amounts of water to adhere fondant decorations.

19. **Glue gun.** I use a glue gun to attach ribbon to my presentation boards.

20. **Scissors.** You'll need these to snip ribbon and cut out template outlines.

21. **Foam flower making pad (shown on page 41).** This is a thick piece of foam used for making fondant flowers.

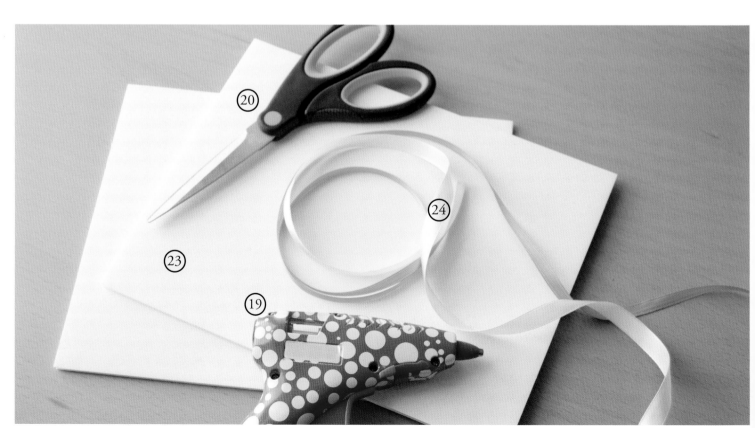

MATERIALS

22. Parchment paper. I always use parchment paper to roll out my gingerbread. It eliminates the need for flour, makes transferring shapes easy, and doesn't stick to the dough.

23. Foam core. Foam core is a sturdy material consisting of a sheet of foam with paper adhered to both sides. It's perfect for both templates and presentation boards.

24. Ribbon. I always keep a collection of narrow ribbon in various colors to give my presentation boards a finished, polished look.

25. Decorating materials. The decorating materials I use most are royal icing, candy, and fondant. Read more about them on pages 14–15.

PRESENTATION BOARDS

You can use a regular foil-covered cake board to display your gingerbread creation, but a handmade presentation board really gives it an added finishing touch. I always make my presentation boards from foam core, which is widely available at craft stores and dollar stores. For small projects, a one-layer board is fine, but for larger projects I always glue together two layers of foam core for added strength.

TO MAKE THE BOARD:

1. For a double board: glue two pieces of foam core together with a glue gun. (You can also use a double-sided tape dispenser to adhere the two pieces.) For a single board: proceed to Step 2.

2. For a rectangular board: measure and cut the foam core to size with a sharp craft knife and a ruler (each project includes appropriate measurements for its presentation board, but a good rule of thumb is to leave about 2" of board space around your project). For a circular board: trace the outline of a circular baking pan with pencil or use a compass to draw a circle, then cut the circle out with a sharp craft knife. (Always use a cutting mat underneath when you're using a craft knife!)

3. Glue a ribbon around the edge of the board and trim off the end. I recommend a ¼" ribbon for a single board and a ³⁄₁₆" ribbon for a double board. Make sure the seam of the ribbon is at the back when you display your project.

DECORATING MATERIALS

Without a doubt, the best part of making a gingerbread creation, whether it be a house or anything else, is decorating it! I use a combination of three main decorating materials—royal icing, candy, and fondant. Decorating adds color, contrast, and detail to your project, and allows you to be as creative as you want. Don't forget to have some extra candy on hand for hungry mouths to snack on along the way—that's part of the fun!

ROYAL ICING

CANDY

ROLLED FONDANT

Royal icing is an extremely important component in gingerbread art. Its consistency can be adjusted from thick to runny, but it always dries hard. It's not only the "glue" that holds gingerbread together—it's also used for outlining and flooding (which gives gingerbread pieces a smooth coat of color), piping designs, and attaching decorations. See pages 30–39 for much more information on royal icing and its uses.

The types of candy you can use to decorate your gingerbread creation are too numerous to list! I like to use classic, simply-shaped candies to accent my designs. You can use the candies I suggest for each project, or replace them with others of your choice. Kids will love choosing their favorite sweets and nibbling on them while they help you decorate—I've been known to do this many times myself!

Rolled fondant is a pliable sugar dough that can be colored, rolled out, and shaped to create many different types of decorations to accent your project, such as balls, rolled ropes, simple flowers, and adorable figurines. Readily available in stores and online, fondant is easy to work with and provides an added level of detail that can't be achieved with candy alone. See pages 40–41 for more information on fondant techniques.

GEL FOOD COLORING
I use gel food coloring for tinting both royal icing and fondant. Gel colors are very concentrated, so most of the time, a little goes a long way. However, some colors, like red, brown, and black, require a larger amount to reach the desired shade.

DUSTING POWDERS
I love using edible dusting powders to add small amounts of color to fondant flowers. These dusts transform a flower from ordinary to extraordinary with just a few dabs of a small paintbrush.

WORKING WITH GINGERBREAD

In this section, you'll learn all about mixing, rolling, cutting, and baking gingerbread dough. Don't be intimidated by the thought of baking gingerbread from scratch; the recipe I use makes a versatile dough that's wonderfully easy to work with. Remember to always bake a few extra pieces—crisp, warm gingerbread straight out of the oven is a treat like no other!

THE MYTHS
OF GINGERBREAD

In my travels down the gingerbread road, I've discovered there are a few very common "gingerbread myths" out there and before we continue, I'd like to try my best to dispel them. Here are the four most common misconceptions:

MYTH #1 - Building a gingerbread structure is difficult.

OK, so if you've never baked or worked with gingerbread before, you might want to start with some of the easier projects in this book. But once you've mastered the basic principles of construction, and practiced the simple piping and decorating techniques, you'll be able to create each and every one of them. The secrets to creating a successful gingerbread structure lie in using the right type of gingerbread and the right type of icing—and I'll be covering both in detail.

MYTH #2 - Gingerbread houses might look pretty, but they taste awful and you risk breaking a tooth if you dare to take a bite of one.

I always use the same recipe, and it's delicious: crisp, not too heavy, and yet strong enough to use for all the projects in this book. Make no mistake, this isn't a soft, chewy cookie; it needs a certain amount of firmness to give the required structural support. But it's far from being the rock-hard, tasteless substance that you'll find in the pre-fabricated boxed gingerbread house sets. I've always gotten rave reviews on it and I know you will too.

MYTH #3 - To build a house that won't collapse, you need to roll out your gingerbread very thickly and use a ton of icing to glue it all together.

Wrong on both counts! As you'll see, I roll my gingerbread quite thinly and use icing sparingly. Thinner, lighter walls are easier to handle and less prone to collapse, and if you use the right consistency of royal icing, you don't need much to hold it all together. The finished look is cleaner, and leaves the focus on the decoration.

MYTH #4 - You can make a gingerbread house from start to finish in just one day.

Building with gingerbread requires a little time and patience. A gingerbread house, or any other kind of three-dimensional gingerbread structure, should be made over at least two days, sometimes three. If the icing isn't given ample time to dry between steps, it can lead to all kinds of problems, including the dreaded "collapse." If you're willing to put in the time, it'll be worth it in the end—and more time just means more gingerbread fun!

OK, so now that we've gotten that out of the way . . . let's get started!

THE INGREDIENTS

Often, gingerbread creations are not eaten right away, but put on display—as they should be, since a lot of work went into creating them! Gingerbread's strength and durability, coupled with the fact that it stays fresh at room temperature for a long period of time, make it a perfect building material. But I feel strongly that if you just happened to break off a piece of your project for a quick snack (hint: if you take it off the back, no one will notice) it should taste **good**.

My gingerbread recipe is adapted from a recipe used by Devon Bakery, formerly located in Manotick, Ontario. Since the first time I tried this recipe, I've never used anything else for any of my gingerbread projects. It's easy to prepare, inexpensive, and strong enough to provide excellent support for any gingerbread structure. It also happens to be just the right combination of sweet and spicy; quite simply, it's delicious! I make a lot of gingerbread, and I end up with a lot of scraps—but trust me, they are never wasted. They're perfect for a quick snack, and my family never gets tired of them.

There are only eight simple ingredients in the gingerbread recipe I use, and all of them are readily available—you probably have most of them in your kitchen cupboards already! I'm often asked about substitutions; I don't recommend them, as I've only ever achieved consistent results with this combination of ingredients. However, there's nothing wrong with experimenting, so feel free to try adjustments if you'd like!

1. FLOUR
All-purpose flour is the main structural ingredient in gingerbread.

2. WATER
A small amount of water adds the extra moisture needed to hold the dough together.

3. SUGAR
Sugar, along with adding sweetness, aids in tenderizing and browning.

4. MOLASSES
Molasses adds a deep flavor to gingerbread dough and also gives it its lovely rich color.

5. SHORTENING
Shortening, a tenderizer, ensures that the gingerbread won't be tough. It's important not to substitute butter for shortening in this recipe.

6. GROUND GINGER
This ground spice gives gingerbread the flavor that made it famous.

7. BAKING SODA
My gingerbread recipe uses only a small amount of leavener to prevent it from puffing and spreading too much.

8. SALT
Salt is an important ingredient that not only balances the sweetness, but enhances gingerbread's flavor and improves its texture as well.

PREPARING
THE DOUGH

One of the reasons I love this recipe so much is that it's so quick to prepare. Also, there are no special tricks to mixing it—I've made it so many times that I think I could make it in my sleep! However, here are a few tips to keep your results consistent.

MEASURING THE INGREDIENTS: I recommend using a kitchen scale to measure your flour, sugar, shortening, and molasses; weighing your ingredients ensures that you measure the exact amounts every time. I've provided measurements in grams and ounces. However, if you don't have a scale, I've also provided amounts in cups.

REFRIGERATING THE DOUGH: Many gingerbread doughs need to be refrigerated before rolling out, but this one doesn't! In fact, it rolls out easier and bakes up more smoothly when it's freshly mixed. Therefore, I recommend making your dough right before you plan to roll it out.

STORING AND REROLLING THE DOUGH: Although it rolls best when it's fresh, that doesn't mean that you can't store unused dough in the refrigerator and keep it for later use. Just wrap it tightly in plastic and refrigerate it for up to two weeks. When you're ready to reuse the dough, bring it to room temperature, break it up into small pieces with your hands or electric mixer, and form it into a ball again—it's ready to reroll.

GINGERBREAD*

200 g / 7 oz. / 1 cup shortening
200 g / 7 oz. / 1 cup granulated sugar
160 g / 5.5 oz. / ½ cup molasses
(regular, not blackstrap)
2 tbsp water
480 g / 17 oz. / 3 cups all-purpose flour
4 tsp ground ginger
1 tsp salt
½ tsp baking soda

(For chocolate gingerbread, add
25 g / 1oz. / ¼ cup of cocoa and a
tbsp of water.)

1. Preheat oven to 350°F.

2. Using a stand mixer with the paddle attachment or a sturdy hand mixer, beat the shortening and sugar together until light and fluffy.

3. Add molasses and water and beat until incorporated. Scrape down bowl and beat again for another 30 seconds.

4. In a separate bowl, sift dry ingredients together and then add all at once to the mixer.

5.

Mix on slow speed until the dry ingredients are incorporated and the dough appears crumbly.

6.

When you press the dough with your hands, it will stick together.

7.

Once the dough has come together firmly in a ball, it's ready to roll out!

Recipe can be halved or doubled. (For all of the projects in this book, I've suggested making one full recipe—it may leave you with extra gingerbread, but it's better to have too much, than too little!)

ROLLING AND
CUTTING THE DOUGH

Rolling out an even sheet of gingerbread is a crucial step in producing smooth, flat cookies. After much trial and error, I've discovered that rolling the dough between two sheets of parchment paper is by far the most effective method. Once the dough is rolled out, shapes are cut directly on the parchment, so that when the excess dough is removed, the entire sheet can be lifted up at once and transferred to the baking tray. Since gingerbread dough doesn't stick to parchment paper, there is no need to use any flour, and because the shapes are baked directly on the parchment, it's not necessary to move them individually and risk warping or damaging the shape. (For various reasons, a few projects require that shapes be transferred after they're rolled and cut. I'll explain why and how to do it in the specific project instructions.)

To help me roll out my dough to exactly the same thickness every time, I place two strips of Plexiglas (I call them thickness strips) on each side of my parchment paper, underneath my rolling pin. Doing this makes it impossible for the rolling pin to roll out the dough any thinner than the strips, and ensures that the sheet of dough is a consistent thickness from one side to the other. I have two sets of strips—one set is ⅛" thick and the other is ¼" thick. I occasionally use the ¼" set, but for the vast majority of my gingerbread projects, I use the ⅛" set. These tools are incredibly handy; I never roll gingerbread dough without them. It's not impossible to roll an even sheet of dough without their help, but they eliminate the guesswork and save a lot of time. Plexiglas sheets are available at home and building stores—ask an attendant to cut the strips to size for you.

If you're working without thickness strips, try to roll your dough to as close as possible to ⅛" thick (except in the rare cases when the project specifies ¼").

ROLLING THE DOUGH

1. Lay a sheet of parchment paper on a flat work surface. The sheet of parchment should be no larger than the size of your baking tray.

2. Transfer the dough from your mixing bowl onto the parchment paper.

3. Place another sheet of parchment paper on top and position your thickness strips on either side.

4. Roll out the gingerbread, occasionally turning your rolling pin to ensure even spread of the dough, until it's reached the same thickness as your strips. Don't worry if the dough has come past the edges of the parchment paper—you can just cut the edges away.

5. Remove the parchment paper, and there you have it—a smooth, even sheet of gingerbread dough ready for cutting shapes!

CUTTING SHAPES

If you're using a cookie cutter:

Place the cutter directly on the dough and push down firmly. Remove the cutter. Cut as many shapes as desired or as the sheet of dough will allow, leaving about ½" of space between the shapes.

If you're using a template:

1. Lightly place your template directly on the rolled-out gingerbread dough (if you press it down too hard the template may stick to the dough). Holding a paring knife at a 45 degree angle, cut around the template. Be sure to use the edge of the knife to cut; using the point of the knife will result in a jagged edge. Remove the template and cut additional shapes as needed, leaving at least ½" of space between them.

2. When all the shapes are cut, use the knife to pick up the excess dough and lift it off the baking sheet. Continue until all the excess dough has been removed (the excess can be gathered together and rolled out again).

3. Holding an edge of each side of the parchment paper, lift and place it directly onto the cookie sheet.

4. The shapes can go straight in the oven! They don't need to be refrigerated first.

BAKING BASICS

Soon, you'll be drooling at the irresistible aroma wafting from your oven—there really is nothing like the smell of gingerbread baking! But before you start baking, make sure you read through this section carefully—the baking process is an important part of a successful gingerbread project.

BAKING TIMES: Baking times for gingerbread depend greatly on the size and thickness of the pieces. For example, a small window shutter will bake much faster than a large roof panel. Therefore, it's always a good idea to bake similar sizes of shapes on the same tray, instead of combining small and large shapes.

A good rule of thumb for doneness is to bake until the edges of the shapes are slightly darker than the middle, but this can vary as well. The three cookies shown are baked to three varying degrees of doneness, giving them a slight difference in color. I like to bake different parts of a gingerbread house a little longer than others—for example, the shingles or roof tiles—it adds character and contrast to the final piece.

I don't usually set a timer for my gingerbread—I prefer to check its doneness visually. However, the chart on the following page may help you get an idea of how long it takes various sizes of shapes to bake.

These approximate baking times are based on a 350°F (175°C) conventional oven and gingerbread that is rolled to ⅛" thick. For ¼" thick gingerbread, add about 3 minutes to the time.

SIZE	BAKING TIME
1"	9–11 minutes
2"	11–13 minutes
3"	12–14 minutes
4"	13–15 minutes
5" or more	14–16 minutes

BUBBLES: While it bakes, the gingerbread will puff up, but it will settle back down again before it's done. When you remove your baking tray from the oven, you may notice some areas where the gingerbread has formed a bubble when it puffed up. Immediately after removing it from the oven, simply pat it down gently with a flat spatula and the bubble will disappear.

MAKE SURE THE EDGES ARE STRAIGHT:
If you're baking shapes for a house or other type of three-dimensional structure, it's important that the sides be as straight as possible. Because the recipe doesn't contain much leavener, the shapes should retain their straight edges and sharp corners for the most part, but occasionally, you'll get a little bit of spread. The best way to ensure that the sides are straight enough is to place the corresponding template on top of the just-baked shape. If you notice any areas where the edges peek out, just trim them off with a paring knife (this must be done directly on the cookie sheet, immediately after the shapes have been removed from the oven, because once they start to cool they'll harden very quickly).

If the pieces have already cooled and you notice an edge that's not straight, gently file it with a lemon zester—it's a great way to smooth it down!

COOLING THE GINGERBREAD:
Once your shapes have been trimmed (if necessary), remove them from the baking sheet and place on a cooling rack. Make sure your cooling rack is completely flat.

STORING THE GINGERBREAD:
Gingerbread stays fresh for a long time, but I always try to bake my gingerbread the day before I build my projects, so that it's as fresh as possible and, once decorated, can be displayed for as long as possible before being eaten. If you bake your gingerbread pieces a day or two before you use them, you can store them at room temperature, uncovered, on a cooling rack. However, if you bake them further in advance than a few days, I recommend stacking and storing the pieces in an airtight container in the fridge to prolong their freshness. Once completed, your gingerbread project will stay fresh, uncovered, for up to three weeks; if it's packaged in cellophane, up to 6 weeks.

HUMIDITY:
Where I live, the winters are cold and dry, and the summers are hot and humid. I make most of my gingerbread in the winter months, so humidity usually isn't a concern. However, I did all the gingerbread work for this book during the summer months, so I saw firsthand how humidity affects my recipe. Molasses is hygroscopic, which means it absorbs moisture from the air—so in high humidity, gingerbread will soften a little. My gingerbread recipe holds up well to humidity and I've never had a structure collapse or sag, but in the event that you experience a lot of softening, here are a few tips to keep your gingerbread firm:

• Overbake the pieces a little—the longer the pieces are baked, the harder they will become.
• Keep your kitchen as cool and dry as possible (use air conditioning and a dehumidifier if possible).
• If you find your pieces have softened during storage, place them back on a baking tray lined with parchment and pop them back in a 350°F (175°C) oven for a minute or two.

DECORATING AND BUILDING

I love everything about the baking process, but for me, the real fun begins when I get out my piping bags, mix up my royal icing, and start to decorate and build my project. I love seeing the individual pieces come to life with color and detail, and I'll never tire of the satisfaction of putting the final touches on my completed project, whether it be simple gingerbread men or a complex house. In the following section, you'll learn all you need to know to successfully decorate and construct your own masterpieces. Remember, practice makes perfect—the more you practice the techniques, the easier they'll become and the happier you'll be with your results.

ROYAL ICING

Have you ever heard the saying "you're the royal icing to my gingerbread?" Okay, I haven't either, but royal icing and gingerbread truly do belong together as perfectly as peanut butter and jelly, milk and cookies, and bacon and eggs. Royal icing is, literally, the "glue" that holds a gingerbread structure together. It can be colored, thinned, and spread on cookies to create a smooth coating, and piped into many different designs, including dots, lines, and leaves. It's also perfect to give the look of soft, fresh snow on a finished house.

Being extremely sweet, royal icing works best with gingerbread in small amounts. The good news is that you don't need heaps of icing to hold gingerbread together. Too much icing can look sloppy, and can even be risky, as the added weight can cause structural problems. I'll show you how to use royal icing to give your structure the stability it needs, while still maintaining a clean and polished look.

The reason royal icing works so well as an edible adhesive is because it dries hard. A soft icing, such as buttercream, wouldn't give a gingerbread house the structural strength it needs. Royal icing is very simple to make, and consists of only three main ingredients—icing sugar, meringue powder, and water. Some royal icing recipes use pasteurized egg whites instead of meringue powder, but I love the fluffy texture that meringue powder gives to the icing.

Piping delicate patterns with royal icing may seem difficult, but don't be intimidated—the projects in this book all use a combination of the same simple piping techniques, which you can master with a little bit of practice. On the following pages, you'll find all the information you need to get started.

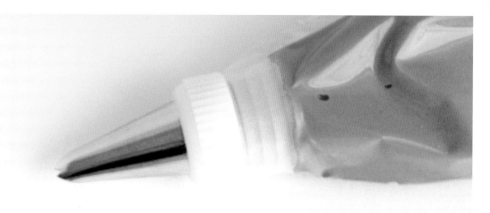

ROYAL ICING*

520 g / 18 oz. / 4 cups icing sugar
3 tbsp meringue powder
8 tbsp water
1 tsp lemon juice (optional)

1. Sift together the icing sugar and meringue powder and add to the bowl of a stand mixer fitted with a paddle attachment.

2. Add water and lemon juice and beat at low speed until combined.

3. Beat at high speed for 5 minutes or until icing forms soft peaks.

4. Add color as desired and use immediately or cover and refrigerate for up to a month. *(See following pages for more information on coloring and storing royal icing.)*

---

* Recipe can be halved or doubled. (For most projects in this book, I've suggested making one full recipe—it may leave you with extra icing, but it's better to have too much, than too little!)

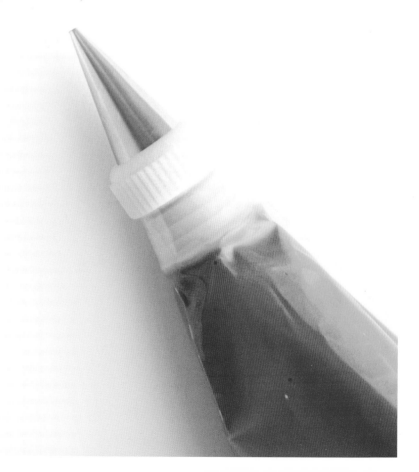

COLORING ROYAL ICING

Royal icing will start to crust immediately if it's not covered. It's important to avoid this because little bits of crusted icing can easily clog piping tips. *(See page 38 for hints on how to prevent and remove clogs.)* I suggest mixing individual colors in glass or plastic mixing bowls with airtight lids so that your royal icing can be covered immediately after the color is added.

1.
Start with freshly beaten royal icing.

2.
Dip a toothpick into the gel color of your choice and dab a small amount on the icing, adding more to deepen the color.*

3.
Stir the icing with a spoon to distribute the color. For large amounts, you can also use a mixer.

4.
When the icing is a uniform color, it's ready to use. Remember to always cover the icing when it's not in use.

* Gel colors are very concentrated—a little goes a long way! However, red, black, and brown may require a significantly greater amount of gel than other colors to achieve the desired depth of color.

STORING ROYAL ICING

You'll often be left with extra royal icing after you've completed a project. Don't throw it away—royal icing stores well (up to a month in the fridge) and can be reused for your next project. Just return any unused icing to an airtight container, refrigerate it, and when you're ready to use it again, give it a quick re-whip with your mixer or a spoon.

Often, while working on projects, you'll need to wait anywhere from a couple of hours to overnight between steps after you've filled your piping bags. While you're not using them, store your piping bags in a resealable plastic bag at room temperature if it's only for a few hours, and in the fridge overnight.

FILLING A PIPING BAG

There's nothing wrong with good high-quality canvas piping bags, but I like to use clear plastic piping bags so that I can easily see what colors are inside. Plastic piping bags are considered disposable, but if you buy good quality ones you can wash and reuse them a few times.

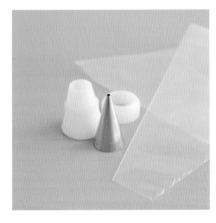

1.
Start with a piping bag (the end of the bag should be snipped off), a coupler set, and the tip of your choice.

2.
Place the coupler insert into the tip of the bag with the narrow end pointing out.

3.
Place a piping tip over the top of the coupler insert.

4.
Place coupler ring over the piping tip and screw into place.

5.
Fold the edges of the bag outward and spoon in the icing (fill no more than halfway).

6.
Twist the end of the bag tightly to seal it. Secure with a rubber band if desired.

PIPING TIPS

Piping is an art form in and of itself. There are many, many piping tips available out there, in a wide variety of sizes, that can create innumerable designs and shapes, but in this book, we only use a small number of very versatile tips and piping techniques that are easy to master. The following tips are all you need to create all the projects in this book.

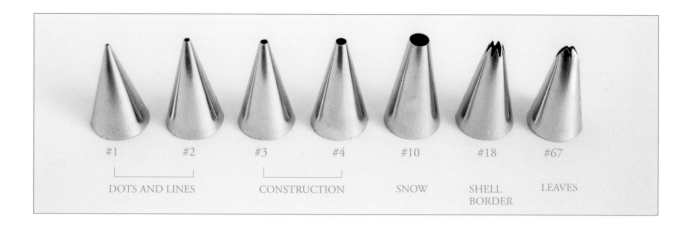

#1   #2   #3   #4   #10   #18   #67

DOTS AND LINES   CONSTRUCTION   SNOW   SHELL   LEAVES
                                                                            BORDER

ICING CONSISTENCY FOR PIPING: It's important for the consistency of your icing to be just right when you pipe designs. If your icing is too thick, your tip may clog easier and lines may break or curl, but if it's too thin, dots, lines, and other patterns may spread and look uneven. Just-mixed royal icing is a perfect consistency for piping lines, but it needs to be thickened slightly for piping certain designs, such as shell borders and leaves. To thicken royal icing, add icing sugar in small amounts; to thin it, add water in small amounts.

(See page 39 for more information on the correct consistency for each of royal icing's uses.)

PIPING TECHNIQUES

STRAIGHT LINES: Much of the piping I do with my gingerbread projects involves variations on lines. It's important to know how to correctly pipe a straight line—once you've mastered that, variations (such as wavy or scalloped lines) will be much easier to do. You'll also be using line piping to outline shapes to prepare them for flooding *(see page 37)*.

The projects almost always specify a #1 tip for line piping, but if you're more comfortable with the slightly larger #2 tip, don't worry, they are interchangeable—you'll just end up with a slightly thicker line.

1.

Start with a piping bag no more than half full, fitted with a #1 or #2 tip. Touch the tip down on your starting point and gently squeeze the piping bag to release a tiny bit of icing.

2.

Gently pull the piping bag upward while putting pressure on the bag and moving it away from the starting point. This will release a continuous line of icing. As you move your bag, the line of icing will fall naturally into place.

3.

Once you've reached your desired end point, touch the tip down and pull away to break the line.

HELPFUL HINTS

• Put pressure on the bag with your dominant hand and use your other hand to guide the bag.

• Try to keep the pressure of the bag and the speed with which you move it consistent. Too little pressure and too much speed can cause the line to break, while too much pressure and too little speed can cause your line to look lumpy and uneven.

• Royal icing is easily removed before it hardens. If you're not happy with your line, just use a toothpick to lift it off the surface and gently scrape away any excess.

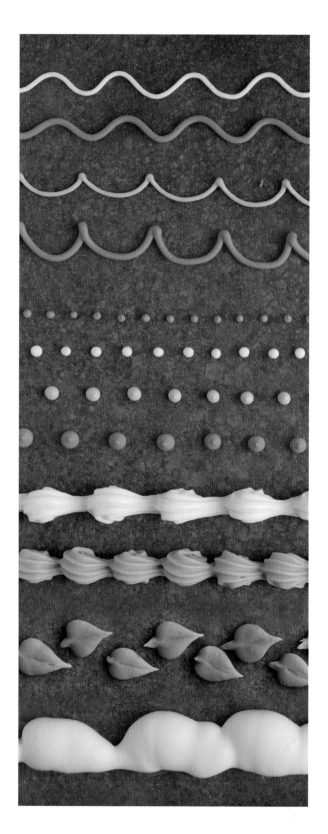

WAVY LINES: Follow the steps for piping a straight line, but move the piping bag up and down as you go, which will release a wavy line. Remember not to touch the tip to the surface of the gingerbread except at the beginning and the end of the line.

SCALLOPED LINE: Touch the tip down on your starting point and gently squeeze the piping bag to release a tiny bit of icing. Put pressure on the bag to release more icing as you move the bag down and then up again, touching the tip down at each point of the scalloped line. Continue until the line is the desired length.

DOTS: Touch the tip down on your starting point and gently squeeze the piping bag to release a tiny bit of icing. Bring the tip up again with a quick motion, cutting off the stream of icing right next to the surface. You can use different sizes of tips to create smaller and larger dots, or you can use the same small tip to pipe both small and larger dots—just release more icing for the larger dots. These four sizes of dots were all piped with a #1 tip.

SHELL BORDER: Touch the tip down on your starting point and squeeze the piping bag to release icing, which will push the tip upward. Move the bag slightly toward you and release the pressure, forming a point. Repeat until your border is the desired length.

LEAVES: Touch the tip down on your starting point and squeeze the piping bag to release the icing, letting it build up at the base of the leaf. Move the bag slightly toward you and release the pressure, forming a point. Repeat for each leaf.

SNOW: Touch the tip down on your starting point and squeeze the piping bag to release the icing. Increase and decrease the pressure on the bag as you move it along, creating "drifts."

FLOODING AN OUTLINE

Flooding is the process of filling a piped outline with thinned royal icing. The icing spreads out and dries evenly, giving gingerbread pieces a smooth, uniform coating. It's great for adding color and contrast to gingerbread projects, and since it dries hard, gives added strength to three-dimensional structures.

Royal icing needs to be thinned with water before flooding, to ensure that it settles and dries evenly. Add small amounts, no more than a teaspoon at a time, until you reach the desired consistency. You'll know it's ready when you stir the icing and it doesn't hold peaks—it should settle down flat again within about 5 to 10 seconds.

FLOODING MEDIUM AND LARGE SHAPES: This is the method I use to flood shapes that are about 3" wide or larger. Use small spoons for the best control—I've used coffee spoons, disposable tasting spoons, and even my kids' old baby spoons!

1.

Pipe an outline on a piece of gingerbread using either a #1 or #2 piping tip. You can proceed immediately to step 2—the outline doesn't have to dry first.

2.

After thinning some of the royal icing, spread it over the surface of the cookie, using a small spoon to push it into the corners. The icing should completely flatten when it settles.

3.

Pop any tiny air bubbles with a toothpick and leave to dry for at least 6 hours or overnight.

FLOODING SMALL SHAPES:
When you're flooding very small shapes, especially ones with sharp corners, using a spoon can get messy and awkward. If the shape is smaller than 3", use the following method.

1.
Pipe an outline on a piece of gingerbread using either a #1 or #2 piping tip. You can proceed immediately to step 2—the outline doesn't have to dry first.

2.
Fill a piping bag no more than halfway with thinned royal icing in the same color as the outline. Pipe a small amount onto the outlined shape.

3.
Spread the icing around the cookie and into the corners using the tip of a toothpick. The icing should completely flatten when it settles. Use the tip of the toothpick to pop any air bubbles and leave to dry for at least 6 hours or overnight.

WHY DOES MY TIP KEEP CLOGGING?

Clogged tips can be really annoying. Since royal icing dries so quickly, small bits can easily get stuck in the nozzle, blocking the steady flow of the icing. Both #1 and #2 tips are prone to clogging because they're so small. To prevent clogs, keep the tips of the piping bags that you're not currently using covered between the folds of a wet towel.

If you do get a clog, remove the coupler ring and the piping tip and push a toothpick through the nozzle of the tip from the inside out—this will force the clog out. Alternately, rinse the tip out thoroughly with warm water to make sure the clog is completely gone.

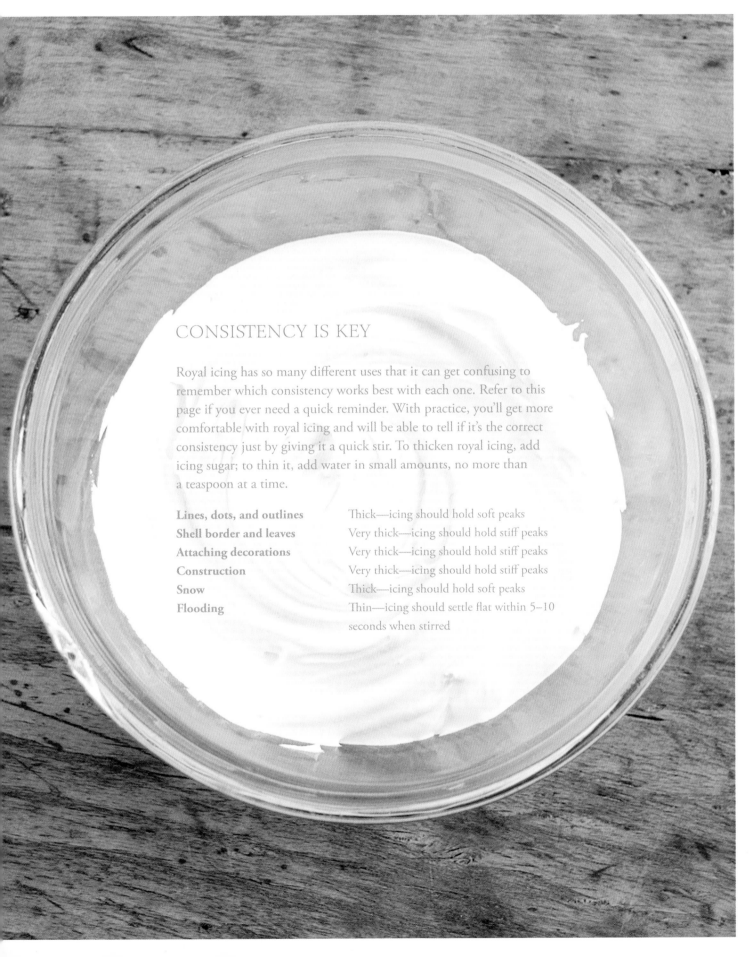

CONSISTENCY IS KEY

Royal icing has so many different uses that it can get confusing to remember which consistency works best with each one. Refer to this page if you ever need a quick reminder. With practice, you'll get more comfortable with royal icing and will be able to tell if it's the correct consistency just by giving it a quick stir. To thicken royal icing, add icing sugar; to thin it, add water in small amounts, no more than a teaspoon at a time.

Lines, dots, and outlines	Thick—icing should hold soft peaks
Shell border and leaves	Very thick—icing should hold stiff peaks
Attaching decorations	Very thick—icing should hold stiff peaks
Construction	Very thick—icing should hold stiff peaks
Snow	Thick—icing should hold soft peaks
Flooding	Thin—icing should settle flat within 5–10 seconds when stirred

ROLLED FONDANT

Candy is great for decorating gingerbread projects, but when I want to create decorations that are a little more detailed and unique, I always use rolled fondant. Fondant is a pliable sugar dough that can be kneaded, molded, or rolled out into just about any shape you can imagine. Many of the projects in this book are enhanced by simple fondant decorations such as balls, ropes, small flowers, birds, and even a cute little alien. You'll find instructions on how to form some basic fondant decorations on the opposite page, while instructions for the more detailed decorations can be found in the individual projects.

Prefabricated fondant is widely available in stores that carry cake decorating products. There are many brands available, all of which are suitable to the uses in this book. I always use Satin Ice fondant because I love its superior quality and taste.

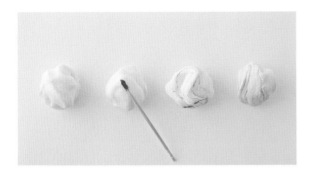

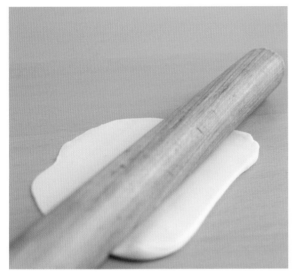

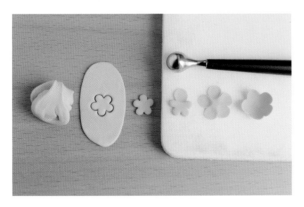

COLORING FONDANT: To color fondant, use a toothpick to add a small amount of gel food coloring to the fondant and knead until the color has been evenly distributed. (Wear plastic gloves if you don't want stained hands!) Always start with small amounts of color—it's much easier to deepen the color than to lighten it. (Red, black, and brown require larger amounts of gel to achieve a deep color—I actually prefer to buy pre-tinted fondant for these three colors.) Fondant will start to dry out when exposed to air, so always wrap it tightly in plastic and store in an airtight container when not in use.

ROLLING OUT FONDANT: Because the amounts of fondant you'll be rolling out for the projects in this book will be small, I recommend using a small rolling pin. You can use either a bit of cornstarch or shortening on your work surface to prevent fondant from sticking when you roll it out. After every few rolls, lift the sheet of fondant up and turn it slightly to ensure it's not sticking to your work surface.

SIMPLE FLOWERS: Roll a small amount of fondant into a sheet about ⅛" thick. Cut a flower shape with a small flower cutter (¼" to ¾") and remove excess. Transfer the flower onto a foam flower making pad and press a ball tool into each petal to form a slight depression. If you'd like your flower to appear more three-dimensional, press the ball tool into the middle of the flower and circle it around, which will automatically lift the petals upward, giving the flower a cupped shape.

ROPES AND TWISTED ROPES: Start with two equal-sized amounts of fondant. With the palms of your hands, roll each into a thin, even rope. Pinch the ropes together at one end and twist them to form a double rope that resembles a candy cane.

BALLS: Roll a small amount of fondant into a thin, even rope. With a sharp knife, cut the rope into even sections and then roll the pieces into balls. This will ensure that all the balls are the same size.

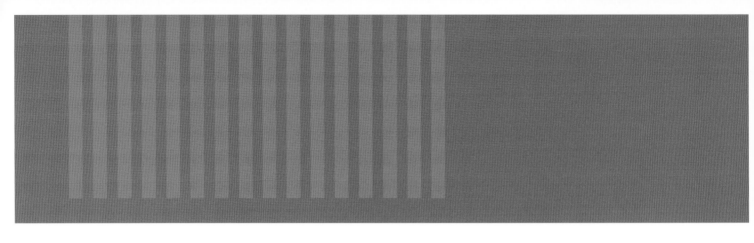

THE BASICS
OF CONSTRUCTION

Though the scope and detail of the three-dimensional projects in this book vary greatly, the basic principles of construction are the same for all. I recommend starting with a simpler project first and moving on to the more complicated ones once you feel comfortable with putting a structure together. Here are some important things to remember before you start constructing:

ALWAYS USE ROYAL ICING TINTED BROWN: In my opinion, nothing takes away more from the look of a finished gingerbread showpiece than a lot of white icing oozing out of the edges. To avoid this, I always use royal icing tinted brown to adhere my pieces together. This way, even if a bit of icing peeks out, it won't be noticeable and will blend in with the color of the gingerbread. Remember that when you tint royal icing brown, you'll need quite a bit of gel color—more than you would for most colors. I recommend about ½ teaspoon of gel color to every 1 cup of royal icing to achieve the desired shade.

DO MOST OF THE DECORATING BEFORE YOU START CONSTRUCTING: Any flooding and/or piping should always be done (and thoroughly dried) before you start putting the structure together. Candy and fondant decorations can be attached either before or after the structure is built (I prefer to attach mine before, and the project instructions reflect this) with the exception of decorations that are attached along a seam—these should always be added after.

USE THE CORRECT CONSISTENCY OF ROYAL ICING: Make sure the royal icing you use for "gluing" is stiff and not runny. Use icing sugar to thicken the icing if necessary.

BUILDING A SIMPLE HOUSE

Before you start building, be sure to read through these steps to building a standard four-walled house with a door. Most of the house projects in the book follow these exact steps (and if they differ at all, I've indicated it in the individual project). Once you familiarize yourself with these steps, the process will start to seem easy. Remember: be patient! The most important part of construction is letting the icing dry sufficiently between steps.

These directions are based on a standard sized gingerbread house, so I've indicated a #4 tip for piping the strips of royal icing to hold it together. A #4 tip is perfect for this size of house and larger, but if you're making a smaller house, you can use a #3 tip, or even #2 for really tiny houses. Again, I've indicated in the individual projects when smaller sizes are appropriate.

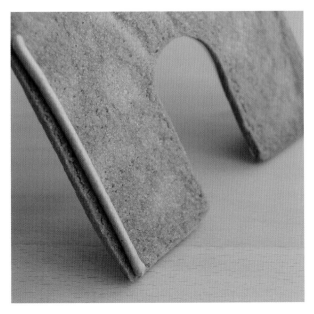

1.

Pipe a strip of icing on the back edge of the front piece using a piping bag fitted with a #4 tip.

2.

Stand the front piece up and attach the corresponding side piece to it. You should be able to let it stand on its own right away.

3.

Pipe a strip of icing along the side edge of the second side panel and attach it to the other side of the front panel.

4.

Pipe a strip of icing along both inside edges of the back panel and attach them to the side panels.

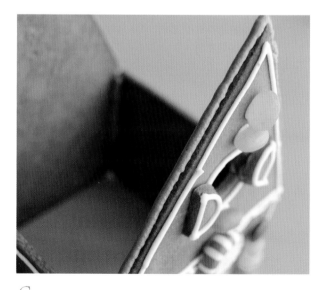

5.

Reinforce the walls by piping thick strips of icing along the inside seams. Let dry for at least 6 hours.

6.

Pipe strips of icing on the top edges of the house where the roof will be attached.

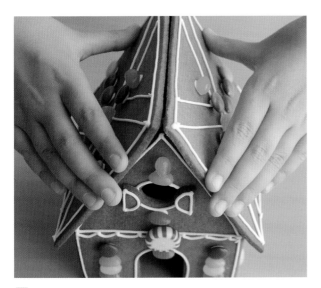

7.

Immediately place roof pieces on the house and hold together gently but firmly, for about 5 minutes, until the icing has set enough so that the pieces will stay on their own.

8.

Pipe a strip of icing along the roof seam for extra reinforcement. Let the house dry overnight.

9.

Gently pick the house up and place on the presentation board. Pipe a strip of icing along the side of the door and attach.

10.

Attach any decorations on the side and roof seams. Pipe snow along the base of the house to attach the house to the board, and along the roof where desired.

PROJECTS

Now that you've read through the first section,
you're ready to get going! You can create all these projects with the skills
you've learned in the previous chapters, but some are easier than others.
Each project is rated on a difficulty level of 1 to 4.

Level 1: A good place to start if you've never worked with gingerbread.
Level 2: You're ready for simple three-dimensional work.
Level 3: You're pretty comfortable with decorating and construction.
Level 4: You're ready for a challenge!

Remember—be patient, have fun, and make sure to eat lots of
gingerbread along the way!

Cookie Puzzles – page 49

Place Cards – page 55

Tree Ornaments – page 61

Candleholder – page 67

Toy Box – page 73

Candy-Filled Houses – page 79

Classic Candy House – page 87

Love Shack – page 93

Birdhouse – page 99

Garden Cottage – page 107

Ice-Cream Parlor – page 113

Haunted House – page 119

Rocket – page 127

Chess Set – page 135

Robot – page 141

Showhome – page 149

COOKIE PUZZLES

Puzzled about what to put in the kids' stockings? Children and adults alike will love these fun cookie puzzles. Packaged in a cellophane bag and tied with a colorful ribbon, they make perfect stocking stuffers, party favors, or hostess gifts. They're also a great way to practice simple piping and flooding techniques.

Yield: 4 cookie puzzles
Difficulty Level: 1
Finished Size: About 5" x 6"

RECIPES

- 1 royal icing recipe *(page 31)*
- 1 gingerbread recipe *(page 23)*

TOOLS

- Scissors
- Pencil and eraser
- Ruler
- Cutting mat
- Craft knife
- Basic baking equipment (stand mixer or sturdy hand mixer, bowls, measuring cups and spoons, sieve, rubber spatula)
- Toothpicks
- Small bowls
- Small spoons
- Airtight plastic containers for storing icing colors
- Rolling pins (large and small)
- 1/8" thickness strips
- Paring knife
- Cookie sheet
- Cooling rack
- Three piping bags and sets of couplers
- Three #1 piping tips

MATERIALS

- Foam core
- Green, blue, black, and orange food coloring gel
- Parchment paper
- Light green, blue, red, orange, and pink jelly beans
- About 2 oz. rolled fondant
- 4 cellophane bags
- Thin ribbon (about 4 feet/1.2 m long), cut into 4 pieces

CUTTERS

- Snowman (about 4" high)
- Christmas tree (about 4" high)

TEMPLATES

The template for this project can be found on page 156.

TECHNIQUES USED

- Making a template *(page 11)*
- Making royal icing *(page 31)*
- Coloring royal icing *(page 32)*
- Storing royal icing *(page 32)*
- Preparing the dough *(page 22)*
- Rolling and cutting the dough *(pages 24–25)*
- Baking basics *(pages 26–27)*
- Filling a piping bag *(page 33)*
- Piping techniques *(pages 35–36)*
- Flooding an outline *(pages 37–38)*
- Coloring, rolling, and shaping rolled fondant *(pages 40–41)*

METHOD

Be sure to read the baking instructions carefully for this project—unlike most of the others, it includes the extra steps of freezing your cut shapes and separating them on the baking sheet.

The following instructions are for two snowman puzzles and two Christmas tree puzzles.

Prepare your templates

(Reference: Making a Template, page 11)

You can use either foam core or thick cardboard to make the template for this project. The template can be found on page 156.

Make royal icing

(Reference: Royal Icing, pages 30–33)

1. Make a full recipe of royal icing *(page 31)*.

2. Divide it roughly into four portions; tint one green, one lighter green, and one light blue. Leave the last portion white.

3. Take a small amount (about a couple of tablespoons) of the white icing and tint it black.

4. Cover each color tightly with plastic wrap or transfer to airtight containers and set aside.

Bake gingerbread pieces

(Reference: Working with Gingerbread, pages 18–27)

1. Make a full recipe of gingerbread dough *(page 23)*.

2. Roll out a sheet of gingerbread between two sheets of parchment paper using ⅛" thickness strips (or if you're not using strips, roll the gingerbread as close as possible to ⅛" thick), and then remove the top parchment paper. Then using the template, cut a rectangle shape. Remove the excess dough from around the rectangle and gather together for rerolling.

3. Place a cookie cutter in the middle of each rectangle, press down firmly, and remove.

4. Place the tip of your paring knife at the outer edge of the cookie cutter shape and draw the knife outward, cutting lines through the dough (a). For the Christmas tree, the lines can be cut randomly; for the snowman, make sure your cuts include two horizontal lines that will separate the bottom half (the snow) from the top (the sky), as seen on page 53.

5. Lift the parchment paper onto a baking sheet and freeze for about 15 minutes.

6. Once the sheet of dough is chilled, gently lift each shape with the tip of your paring knife and separate them from each other on the baking sheet. Each shape should be at least ½" apart (b).

7. Bake according to the guidelines on pages 26–27.

8. Let the pieces cool completely.

9. Repeat steps 2–8 until you have 4 puzzles baked.

FOR THE CHRISTMAS TREE:

Prepare your piping bags

(Reference: Filling a Piping Bag, page 33)

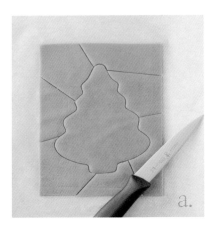

a.

b.

1. Prepare two pastry bags with couplers and #1 tips.

2. Fill one with green royal icing and one with light green royal icing, reserving about half of each.

Outline and flood the shapes

(Reference: Piping Techniques, pages 35–36; Flooding an Outline, pages 37–38)

1. Pipe an outline of green royal icing on the Christmas tree. Pipe a lighter green outline on the rest of the shapes.

2. Thin the reserved green and light green royal icing with small amounts of water (no more than one teaspoon at a time) until you reach the desired flooding consistency.

3. Flood the Christmas tree shape with matching darker green royal icing. Flood the other shapes with the corresponding lighter green royal icing.

4. Let the icing set for about an hour.

Decorate the tree

(Reference: Piping Techniques, pages 35–36)

1. Using the photo as a guide, pipe an outline around the tree and a zigzag pattern from the top to the bottom with light green royal icing.

2. Cut light green, blue, red, and orange jellybeans in half and attach to the tree with a dot of royal icing.

3. Let all pieces dry overnight.

FOR THE SNOWMAN:

Prepare your piping bags

(Reference: Filling a Piping Bag, page 33)

1. Prepare three piping bags with couplers and #1 tips.

2. Fill one with light blue royal icing, one with white royal icing, and one with black royal icing, reserving about half of each.

Outline and flood the shapes

(Reference: Piping Techniques, pages 35–36; Flooding an Outline, pages 37–38)

1. Pipe an outline of white royal icing on the snowman and the bottom "snow" pieces. Pipe a blue outline on the top "sky" pieces. Pipe a black outline for the snowman's hat.

2. Thin the reserved white, blue, and black royal icing with small amounts of water (no more than one teaspoon at a time) until you reach the desired flooding consistency.

3. Flood the snowman shape and the snow shapes with white royal icing, the sky shapes with blue royal icing, and the snowman's hat with the black royal icing.

4. Let the icing set for about an hour.

Decorate the background and the snowman

(Reference: Piping Techniques, pages 35–36; Rolled Fondant, pages 40–41)

1. Pipe dots of white royal icing on the blue shapes to represent snowflakes.

2. Cut pink, orange, and blue jellybeans in half and attach to the snowman's front with a dot of royal icing.

3. To make the scarf:

a) Tint a 1-oz. piece of fondant green and roll out to about ¹⁄₁₆" thick. Cut a strip about ⅓" wide and lay over the snowman's neck, attaching with a bit of white royal icing. Pinch together in the middle and trim off the excess at the sides.

b) Cut another strip of green fondant about ⅓" wide and 2½" long. Pinch one end and using a small paintbrush, attach to the first piece with a tiny dab of water.

c) Cut a small piece of green fondant about ¼" wide and ⅛" long. Place on top of the second piece of fondant, using a tiny dab of water to attach. Gently press the sides of the piece into a curve to give the appearance of the scarf being tied.

4. To make the carrot nose:

a) Tint a half-ounce piece of fondant orange. (You only need a really tiny piece of fondant to make the nose. I recommend saving the unused portion for a later project.) Take a piece of the orange fondant about the size of a small pea and shape it into a pointed cone.

b) Attach the nose to the snowman's face using a small dot of white royal icing.

5. Let all pieces dry completely. Package in bags and tie with ribbons.

Step 3

a.   b.   c.

Step 4

a. & b.

PLACE CARDS

Make every guest feel like the guest of honor when they come to the table and see these personalized place cards. I've provided instructions for four designs that can be easily mixed and matched, but the scope for creativity is endless with this project—you can keep the design and color scheme consistent to match your table decor, or shake things up and make everyone's place card a little bit different.

Yield: 12 place cards
Difficulty Level: 2
Finished Size: About 3½" tall

RECIPES

- 1 royal icing recipe *(page 31)*
- 1 gingerbread recipe *(page 23)*

TOOLS

- Basic baking equipment (stand mixer or sturdy hand mixer, bowls, measuring cups and spoons, sieve, rubber spatula)
- Toothpicks
- Small bowls
- Small spoons
- Airtight plastic containers for storing icing colors
- Rolling pins (large and small)
- ⅛" thickness strips
- Paring knife
- Cookie sheet
- Cooling rack
- Four piping bags and sets of couplers
- Four #1 piping tips
- Edible ink pen

MATERIALS

- Brown, red, and black food coloring gel
- Parchment paper
- Red, green, and blue mini candy-coated chocolate pieces
- Green jelly beans
- Orange and pink small round gumdrops
- About 2 oz. rolled fondant

CUTTERS

- Gingerbread people (about 3" high)
- 2" x 2" square cutter with scalloped edges

TECHNIQUES USED

- Making royal icing *(page 31)*
- Coloring royal icing *(page 32)*
- Storing royal icing *(page 32)*
- Preparing the dough *(page 22)*
- Rolling and cutting the dough *(pages 24–25)*
- Baking basics *(pages 26–27)*
- Filling a piping bag *(page 33)*
- Piping techniques *(pages 35–36)*
- Flooding an outline *(pages 37–38)*
- Coloring, rolling, and shaping rolled fondant *(pages 40–41)*

METHOD

DAY 1

Make royal icing

(Reference: Royal Icing, pages 30–33)

1. Make a full recipe of royal icing *(page 31)*.

2. Divide it roughly into four portions. Tint one brown, one red, and one black. Leave the last portion white.

3. Cover each color tightly with plastic wrap or transfer to airtight containers and set aside.

Bake gingerbread pieces

(Reference: Working with Gingerbread, pages 18–27)

1. Make a full recipe of gingerbread dough *(page 23)*.

2. Roll out a sheet of gingerbread between two sheets of parchment paper using ⅛" thickness strips (or if you're not using strips, roll the gingerbread as

close as possible to ⅛" thick), and then remove top parchment paper. Then cut shapes. For 10 place cards, you'll need:

- **10 gingerbread people**
- **10 2"x 2" scalloped squares**

3. Bake according to the guidelines on pages 26–27.

4. Let the pieces cool completely.

5. Repeat steps 2 through 4 until all the pieces are baked.

Prepare your piping bags

(Reference: Filling a Piping Bag, page 33)

1. Prepare four piping bags with couplers and #1 tips.

2. Fill one with white royal icing, one with red royal icing, one with brown royal icing, and one with black royal icing.

Outline and flood the squares

(Reference: Piping Techniques, pages 35–36; Flooding an Outline, pages 37–38)

1. Outline the squares with white royal icing.

2. Thin the reserved white royal icing with small amounts of water (no more than one teaspoon at a time) until you reach the desired flooding consistency.

3. Flood the squares and let them dry for about an hour.

Decorate the gingerbread people and the squares

(Reference: Piping Techniques, pages 35–36)

FOR PLACE CARD #1:

1. Using the illustration on the following page as a guide, pipe a "stitch" outline and dots and lines for the gingerbread man's cuffs, buttons, necktie, smile, cheeks, and eyes.

2. Attach two pieces of red mini candy-coated chocolate pieces to his toes with a small dot of brown royal icing.

3. For the hat, cut a green jellybean in half lengthwise, and attach it to the top of the gingerbread man's head with a small dot of brown royal icing. Let set for a few minutes, then switch your piping tip on the piping bag with white royal icing, to a #3 tip and pipe a line around the base of the hat from one side to the other. Pipe a dot of white royal icing on the top for the pom pom.

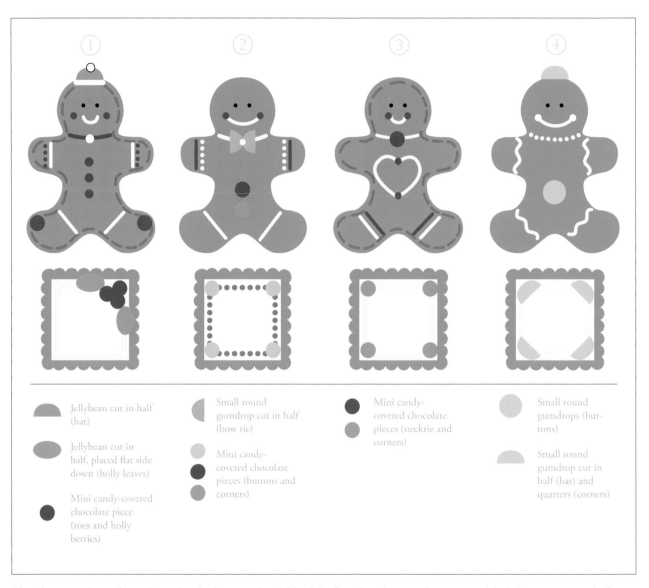

Jellybean cut in half (hat)

Jellybean cut in half, placed flat side down (holly leaves)

Mini candy-covered chocolate piece (toes and holly berries)

Small round gumdrop cut in half (bow tie)

Mini candy-covered chocolate pieces (buttons and corners)

Mini candy-covered chocolate pieces (necktie and corners)

Small round gumdrops (buttons)

Small round gumdrop cut in half (hat) and quarters (corners)

This diagram shows how the individual pieces should look before the place cards are assembled. Use it as a guide for piping lines and dots, and for placing candies.

4. For the square, pipe an outline of white royal icing on top of the white flooded area and pipe a dot at each corner except the top right.

5. Attach three mini red candy-coated pieces to the top right corner of the square with white royal icing.

6. Cut a green jellybean in half lengthwise and attach each half

face down on either side of the red "berries." Let both pieces dry completely overnight.

FOR PLACE CARD #2:

1. Using the illustration and photos as a guide, pipe dots and lines for the gingerbread man's cuffs, necktie, smile, cheeks, and eyes.

2. Attach two pieces of mini candy-coated chocolate for buttons with a small dot of brown royal icing.

3. Cut a small round gumdrop in half and attach with curved ends facing each other for his bow tie. Pipe a dot of white royal icing in the middle.

4. For the square, pipe red dots around the edges of the white

flooded area and attach blue mini candy-coated chocolates to the corners. Let both pieces dry completely overnight.

FOR PLACE CARD #3:

1. Using the illustration and photos as a guide, pipe a "stitch" outline and dots and lines for the gingerbread man's cuffs, heart, necktie, smile, cheeks, and eyes.

2. Attach a piece of mini candy-coated chocolate to his necktie with a small dot of brown royal icing.

3. For the square, pipe an outline of white royal icing on top of the white flooded area and attach a piece of mini candy-coated chocolate to each corner. Let both pieces dry completely overnight.

FOR PLACE CARD #4:

1. Using the illustration and photos as a guide, pipe dots and lines for the gingerbread lady's cuffs, necklace, smile, cheeks, and eyes.

2. Attach one small round gumdrop for a button with a small dot of brown royal icing.

3. For the hat, cut a small round gumdrop in half and attach it to the top of her head with a small dot of brown royal icing.

4. For the square, pipe white dots around the edges of the white flooded area. Cut a small round gumdrop in half and then in half again, and attach flat side down

to each corner. Let both pieces dry completely overnight.

DAY 2

Write names and assemble the place cards

1. With an edible ink pen, write the names of your guests on the squares. (You could also pipe the names onto the squares if you don't have an edible ink pen.)

2. With a piping bag fitted with a #3 tip, pipe brown royal icing along the top edge of the back of the square. (Because it won't show, you can be

generous with the royal icing in this step.)

3. Attach the square to the gingerbread person with both pieces slightly angled toward each other to create a tent card effect *(see photo below)*. Hold them in place for about two minutes; the place card should then be able to stand on its own.

4. Repeat steps 1 through 3 for the other place cards. Let the pieces dry for at least 6 hours before moving them.

To ensure that the two pieces adhere properly, the square card needs to lay flat against the gingerbread person. Avoid placing candies any higher than the gingerbread person's torso, or it might interfere with construction.

TREE ORNAMENTS

These diminutive tree ornaments are only two inches tall, making them the perfect project for the miniature enthusiast. Don't be intimidated by their small size though—it actually makes them easier to assemble. The four designs shown here follow the same color scheme but each have a different roof pattern, giving them a charming individuality. A set of four packaged together in a box makes a memorable gift.

Yield: 8 ornaments
Difficulty Level: 2
Finished Size: About 2" high

WHAT YOU'LL NEED

RECIPES

- 1 royal icing recipe *(page 31)*
- 1 gingerbread recipe *(page 23)*

TOOLS

- Scissors
- Pencil and eraser
- Ruler
- Cutting mat
- Craft knife
- Basic baking equipment (stand mixer or sturdy hand mixer, bowls, measuring cups and spoons, sieve, rubber spatula)
- Toothpicks
- Small bowls
- Small spoons
- Airtight plastic containers for storing icing colors

- Rolling pin (large)
- ⅛" thickness strips
- Paring knife
- Cookie sheet
- Cooling rack
- Four piping bags and sets of couplers
- Three #1 piping tips
- One #3 piping tip

MATERIALS

- Cardboard or heavy paper
- Brown, red, and green food coloring gel
- Parchment paper
- Green ring candies (at least 4; I recommend having a few extras on hand in case of breakage)
- Thin red ribbon (about 4 feet / 1.2m long)

CUTTERS

- 2" x 2" square cutter with scalloped edges (or, if you don't have this cutter, you can use the template equivalent)
- ¾" circle cutter for the door (or you can use the base of a regular piping tip)

TEMPLATES

The templates for this project can be found on page 157.

TECHNIQUES USED

- Making a template *(page 11)*
- Making royal icing *(page 31)*
- Coloring royal icing *(page 32)*
- Storing royal icing *(page 32)*

- Preparing the dough *(page 22)*
- Rolling and cutting the dough *(pages 24–25)*
- Baking basics *(pages 26–27)*

- Filling a piping bag *(page 33)*
- Piping techniques *(pages 35–36)*
- Flooding an outline *(pages 37–38)*
- Construction basics *(pages 42–45)*

METHOD

DAY 1

Prepare your templates

(Reference: Making a Template, page 11)

Since all the pieces for these ornaments are so small, I recommend cutting the templates from a thinner material than foam core, such as heavy cardboard or thick paper. The templates for this project can be found on page 157.

Make royal icing

(Reference: Royal Icing, pages 30–33)

1. Make a full recipe of royal icing *(page 31)*.

2. Divide it roughly into thirds; tint one third brown and one third red.

3. Divide the third amount in half and tint one portion green. Leave the last portion white.

4. Cover each color tightly with plastic wrap or transfer to air-tight containers and set aside.

Bake gingerbread pieces

(Reference: Working with Gingerbread, pages 18–27)

1. Make a full recipe of gingerbread dough *(page 23)*.

2. Roll out a sheet of gingerbread between two sheets of parchment paper using ⅛" thickness strips (or if you're not using strips, roll the gingerbread as close as possible to ⅛" thick), then cut shapes. For 8 ornaments, you'll need:

- **8 front pieces with door cutout** *(see page 91 for instructions on cutting a door)*
- **8 back pieces**
- **8 base pieces (using the 2"x 2" square cutter with scalloped edges)**
- **16 roof pieces**
- **16 side pieces**

3. Bake according to the guidelines on pages 26–27.

4. Let the pieces cool completely.

5. Repeat steps 2 through 4 until all the pieces are baked.

Prepare your piping bags

(Reference: Filling a Piping Bag, page 33)

1. Prepare three piping bags with couplers and #1 tips, and one piping bag with a coupler and a #3 tip.

2. Fill the #3 tip bag with brown roy-

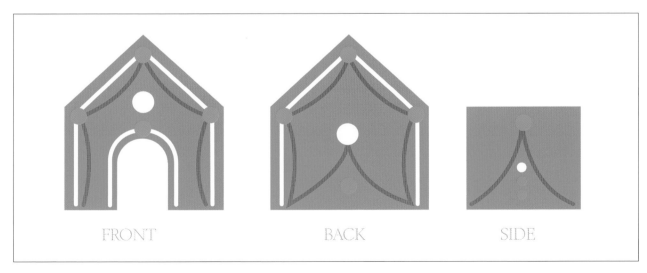

FRONT   BACK   SIDE

This diagram shows how the individual front, back, and side pieces should look before the ornaments are assembled (roof patterns can be found on the following page). Use it as a guide for piping lines and dots.

ROOF

Build the walls

(Reference: The Basics of Construction, pages 42–45)

1. Prepare a piping bag with a coupler and a #3 tip and fill with brown royal icing.

2. Pipe a strip of icing on the back edge of a front piece.

3. Stand the front piece on top of a base piece and attach the corresponding side piece to it. You should be able to let it stand on its own right away.

4. Pipe a strip of brown royal icing along the inside bottom edges of the two panels, to secure them to the base.

5. Pipe a strip of royal icing along the side edge of the second side panel and attach it to the other side of the front panel.

al icing. Fill the other bags with the white, green, and red royal icing, reserving about half of the red royal icing and setting aside.

Outline and flood the roof pieces

(Reference: Piping Techniques, pages 35–36; Flooding an Outline, pages 37–38)

1. Outline the roof pieces with red royal icing.

2. Thin reserved red royal icing with small amounts of water (no more than one teaspoon at a time) until you reach the desired flooding consistency.

3. Flood the roof pieces and let dry for about an hour.

Pipe designs on the side and roof pieces

(Reference: Piping Techniques, pages 35–36)

1. Using the illustrations on the previous page and the photos as a guide, pipe the designs onto the front, back, and side pieces, starting with the white lines, then the red lines, and finishing with the green and white dots. Set aside.

2. Using the illustration above as a guide, pipe lines and dots onto the roof pieces. (You should have four of each pattern.)

3. Let all pieces dry completely overnight.

TRY THIS!

Kids love anything personalized. Instead of patterns, pipe their initials on the side and hide a foil-wrapped chocolate coin in each ornament before you attach the roof pieces.

6. Pipe a strip of royal icing along both inside edges of the back panel and attach them to the side panels.

7. Secure the walls to the base piece with royal icing along the inside, and reinforce the inside wall seams with a strip of royal icing as well.

8. Repeat steps 2 through 7 for the rest of the ornaments. Let them all dry for at least an hour (with a larger house, you'd need a longer drying time for this step, but since these walls won't be supporting a lot of weight, an hour is sufficient).

Attach the roofs

1. Pipe a strip of brown royal icing along the top edges of the walls where the roof pieces will be attached.

2. Immediately place the roof pieces on the house and hold together gently but firmly, for about two

minutes or until the icing has set enough so that the pieces will stay on their own. (Again, since these houses are so small, they don't require quite as long for this step as larger houses do.)

3. Repeat steps 1 and 2 for the rest of the ornaments. Let dry for about an hour.

Attach the ring candy loops

1. With a sharp paring knife or craft knife, firmly press down in the middle of a piece of green ring candy until it splits in half. Repeat this step until you have 8 halves.

2. Pipe a dab of royal icing on both bottom ends of a piece of ring candy, and attach to the roof of an ornament *(see below photo)*.

3. Repeat step 2 for the rest of the ornaments. Let the ornaments dry overnight.

Add the ribbon loops

1. Cut 8 pieces of thin red ribbon about 6" long.

2. Thread the ribbon through the middle of the candy ring and tie the ends tightly in a knot. Trim the ends of the knot to even lengths.

3. Package or display as desired.

HELPFUL TIP

If you end up with leftover royal icing, don't throw it out! Royal icing keeps for a few weeks in the fridge. Use any leftovers for your next project!

CANDLEHOLDER

This gingerbread village candleholder makes a gorgeous centerpiece for your holiday table. The individual pieces are simple to decorate, but when grouped together, they create an elaborate effect.

Glass candleholders are inexpensive and easy to find—this one came from the dollar store! And since everything is attached with royal icing, it can be easily cleaned and reused.

Yield: 1 candleholder
Difficulty Level: 1
Finished Size: About 6" high

RECIPES

- 1 royal icing recipe *(page 31)*
- 1 gingerbread recipe *(page 23)*

TOOLS

- Scissors
- Pencil and eraser
- Ruler
- Cutting mat
- Craft knife
- Basic baking equipment (stand mixer or sturdy hand mixer, bowls, measuring cups and spoons, sieve, rubber spatula)
- Toothpicks
- Small bowls
- Small spoons
- Airtight plastic containers for storing icing colors
- Rolling pin (large)
- ⅛" thickness strips
- Paring knife
- Cookie sheet
- Cooling rack
- Five piping bags and sets of couplers
- Five #1 piping tips
- Two #3 piping tips

MATERIALS

- Cardboard or heavy paper
- Blue, red, green, and brown food coloring gel
- Parchment paper
- Assorted colors of jelly beans (red, green, yellow)
- Cylindrical glass candleholder (or vase) about 3¾" in diameter and 5" tall
- Candle

CUTTERS

- Miniature Christmas tree

TEMPLATES

The templates for this project can be found on page 158.

- Making a template *(page 11)*
- Making royal icing *(page 31)*
- Coloring royal icing *(page 32)*
- Storing royal icing *(page 32)*
- Preparing the dough *(page 22)*
- Rolling and cutting the dough *(pages 24–25)*
- Baking basics *(pages 26–27)*
- Filling a piping bag *(page 33)*
- Piping techniques *(pages 35–36)*
- Flooding an outline *(pages 37–38)*

METHOD

DAY 1

Prepare your templates

(Reference: Making a Template, page 11)

Since the house shapes for this project are small, I recommend cutting the templates from a thinner material than foam core, such as heavy cardboard or thick paper. The templates for this project can be found on page 158.

The circle template's curved edge makes it difficult to cut from foam core as well, so I recommend that it also be cut from a thinner material.

Make royal icing

(Reference: Royal Icing, pages 30–33)

1. Make a full recipe of royal icing (page 31).

2. Divide it roughly into five portions; tint one portion blue, one red, one green, and one brown. Leave the last portion white.

3. Divide the green into two portions and add more gel color to one to make a darker green.

4. Cover each color tightly with plastic wrap or transfer to airtight containers and set aside.

Bake gingerbread pieces

(Reference: Working with Gingerbread, pages 18–27)

1. Make a full recipe of gingerbread dough (page 23).

2. Roll out a sheet of gingerbread between two sheets of parchment paper using ⅛" thickness strips (or if you're not using strips, roll the gingerbread as close as possible to ⅛" thick), and then remove top parchment paper. Then cut shapes. You'll need:

   • **1 base circle shape***
   • **4 large house shapes**
   • **4 medium house shapes**
   • **4 small house shapes**
   • **8 tree shapes**

   * The size of the base circle corresponds to the size of the candleholder I used. If you're unable to find a candleholder exactly that size, you might need to slightly increase or decrease the size of the base circle. A good rule of thumb is to make sure the diameter of the base circle is at least 2" larger than the diameter of the candleholder.

3. Bake according to the guidelines on pages 26–27.

4. Let the pieces cool completely.

5. Repeat steps 2 through 4 until all the pieces are baked.

TRY THIS!

This candleholder does double duty as decoration and dessert! Display it during the meal, then invite guests to break a piece off to nibble on afterward.

Prepare your piping bags

(Reference: Filling a Piping Bag, page 33)

1. Prepare five piping bags with couplers and #1 tips.

2. Fill one with white royal icing, one with red royal icing, one with blue royal icing, one with the lighter green royal icing and one with the darker green royal icing, reserving about half of each color. Make sure to cover the reserved portions while not in use.

Outline and flood the shapes

(Reference: Piping Techniques, pages 35–36; Flooding an Outline, pages 37–38)

1. Pipe an outline around the circle shape with white royal icing.

2. Pipe an outline around the tree shapes with the darker green royal icing.

Jellybean cut in
half lengthwise

Jellybean cut in
half widthwise

This diagram shows how the individual pieces should look before the candleholder is assembled. Use it as a guide for piping lines and dots, and for placing candies.

3. Pipe outlines around the house shapes, half with the lighter green royal icing and half with the blue royal icing. You can either outline the whole shape, or just the roof; an assortment of each looks best.

4. Thin the reserved white royal icing with small amounts of water (no more than one teaspoon at a time) until you reach the desired flooding consistency.

5. Flood the circle shape with the thinned white royal icing and set aside.

6. Repeat steps 4 and 5 for the blue and both shades of green royal icing. Flood all the shapes with their corresponding colors. Set aside and let dry for about an hour.

Decorate the house and tree shapes

(Reference: Piping Techniques, pages 35–36)

FOR THE HOUSES:

1. Using the illustration and photos as a guide, pipe dots and outlines to create the roof and door details.

2. Cut jellybeans in half lengthwise and widthwise and attach to the house shapes with a small dot of royal icing.

3. Let dry completely overnight.

FOR THE TREE:

1. Using the illustration and photos as a guide, pipe blue, red, and white "lights" on the tree and a larger white "star" at the top.

2. Let dry completely overnight.

DAY 2

Prepare your piping bags

1. Prepare two piping bags with couplers and #3 tips.

2. Fill one with white royal icing and one with brown royal icing.

Assemble the village

1. Make sure the candleholder is clean and free of fingerprints.

2. Pipe a large dot of white royal icing in the middle of the base piece. (Because it won't show, you can be generous with the royal icing in this step.) Place the candleholder on top (a).

3. Attach the house shapes to the sides of the candleholder with large dots of brown royal icing.

Vary the placement so that the large houses alternate with the medium and small houses (b).

4. Continue attaching the house shapes until they reach all the way around the perimeter. Add the remaining houses in front of the first layer to create a three-dimensional effect.

5. Attach the trees in front of the house shapes with large dots of brown royal icing (c).

Add the "snow"

1. With a piping bag fitted with a #3 tip, pipe white royal icing on the tops of the houses and trees and a bit around the bottom to give the effect of fallen snow (d).

2. Let the whole village dry for at least 6 hours before moving it, or inserting the candle.

a.

b.

c.

d.

TOY BOX

These miniature toy boxes are so adorable. They're perfect little gifts for the holidays, as well as baby showers, birthdays, and christenings. It's a great beginner three-dimensional construction project—the rectangle shapes for the box are easy to cut and the box's small size makes it easy to assemble. Miniature cookie cutters are widely available at stores where cake decorating supplies are sold.

Yield: 2 toy boxes
Difficulty Level: 2
Finished Size: About 3½" high

RECIPES

- 1 royal icing recipe *(page 31)*
- 1 gingerbread recipe *(page 23)*

TOOLS

- Scissors
- Pencil and eraser
- Ruler
- Cutting mat
- Craft knife
- Basic baking equipment (stand mixer or sturdy hand mixer, bowls, measuring cups and spoons, sieve, rubber spatula)
- Toothpicks
- Small bowls
- Small spoons
- Airtight plastic containers for storing icing colors

- Rolling pins (large and small)
- ⅛" thickness strips
- Paring knife
- Cookie sheet
- Cooling rack
- Six piping bags and sets of couplers
- Five #1 piping tips
- One #3 piping tip
- One #10 piping tip

MATERIALS

- Foam core or thick cardboard
- Blue, red, yellow, black, and brown food coloring gel
- Parchment paper
- About 3 oz. rolled fondant
- Plastic wrap

CUTTERS

- Assorted miniature cutters (teddy bear, ball, train, airplane, spinning top, and small star)
- Letter cutters

TEMPLATES

The templates for this project can be found on page 157.

- Making a template *(page 11)*
- Making royal icing *(page 31)*
- Coloring royal icing *(page 32)*
- Storing royal icing *(page 32)*
- Preparing the dough *(page 22)*

- Rolling and cutting the dough *(pages 24–25)*
- Baking basics *(pages 26–27)*
- Filling a piping bag *(page 33)*
- Piping techniques *(pages 35–36)*

- Flooding an outline *(pages 37–38)*
- Coloring, rolling, and shaping rolled fondant *(pages 40–41)*
- Construction basics *(pages 42–45)*

METHOD

DAY 1

Prepare your templates

(Reference: Making a Template, page 11)

You can use either foam core or thick cardboard to make the templates for this project. The templates can be found on page 157.

Make royal icing

(Reference: Royal Icing, pages 30–33)

1. Make a full recipe of royal icing *(page 31)*.

2. Divide it roughly into six portions; tint one portion light blue, one red, one light yellow, one black, and one brown. Leave the last portion white.

3. Cover each color tightly with plastic wrap or transfer to airtight containers and set aside.

Bake gingerbread pieces

(Reference: Working with Gingerbread, pages 18–27)

1. Make a full recipe of gingerbread dough *(page 23)*.

2. Divide the recipe in half and wrap one portion tightly in plastic wrap; refrigerate for use in another project.

3. Roll out a sheet of gingerbread between two sheets of parchment paper using ⅛" thickness strips (or if you're not using strips, roll the gingerbread as close as possible to ⅛" thick), and then remove top parchment paper. Then cut shapes. To make two toy boxes, you'll need:

   - **About 25 miniature cookies (cut 5 of each shape)**
   - **2 front pieces**
   - **2 back pieces**
   - **4 side pieces**
   - **2 base pieces**
   - **2 lid pieces**

4. Bake according to the guidelines on pages 26–27.

5. Let the pieces cool completely.

6. Repeat steps 3 through 5 until all the pieces are baked.

Prepare your piping bags

(Reference: Filling a Piping Bag, page 33)

1. Prepare five piping bags with couplers and #1 tips, and one piping bag with couplers and a #3 tip.

2. Fill the #3 tip bag with brown royal icing. Fill the other bags with the white, red, blue, yellow, and black icing. Make sure to cover the reserved portions while not in use.

Outline and flood the toy shapes

(Reference: Piping Techniques, pages 35–36; Flooding an Outline, pages 37–38)

1. Pipe outlines around the airplane shapes with white royal icing.

2. Pipe outlines around the circle shapes with yellow royal icing.

3. Pipe outlines around the spinning top shapes with red royal icing.

4. Pipe outlines around the train shapes with blue royal icing.

5. Thin the reserved portions of white, yellow, blue, and red royal icing with small amounts of water (no more than one teaspoon at a time) until you reach the desired flooding consistency.

Use this illustration as a guide to decorate the miniature cookies.

6. Flood all the shapes with their corresponding colors. Set aside and let dry for about an hour.

Tint your rolled fondant and decorate the shapes

(Reference: Piping Techniques, pages 35–36, and Rolled Fondant, pages 40–41)

1. Tint three 1-oz. pieces of rolled fondant—one light blue, one green, and one red (red can be difficult to tint; I recommend using pre-tinted red fondant).

TRY THIS!

For a quicker project, make a mini pirate's chest instead of a toy box. Just drop the letters from the front of the box and fill it with candy and gold coins—yum!

FOR THE TRAINS:

1. Roll out the red fondant to about ¹⁄₁₆" thick. Using a #10 tip, cut circles and attach to the trains for wheels. Cut small rectangles and attach to the top of the trains.

FOR THE SPINNING TOPS:

1. Roll out the blue fondant to about ¹⁄₁₆" thick. Cut strips about ¼" wide and lay them over the top, curving slightly to give a three dimensional effect. Secure with a small dot of royal icing and trim the edges.

2. Pipe handles for the tops with yellow royal icing.

FOR THE TEDDY BEARS:

1. Pipe a muzzle on the bears with brown royal icing. Pipe dots of black royal icing for their nose and eyes.

FOR THE BALLS:

1. Tint a 1-oz. piece of fondant green and roll out to about ¹⁄₁₆" thick. Cut strips about ¼" wide and lay over the balls, curving slightly to give a three-dimensional effect. Secure with a small dot of royal icing and trim the edges.

2. Roll out a 1-oz. piece of red fondant to about ¹⁄₁₆" thick. Cut star shapes and attach to the tops of the balls with a small dot of royal icing, trimming off the top two points. (If you don't have a small star cutter, you can pipe the star onto the shape.)

FOR THE AIRPLANES:

1. Pipe dots and lines of blue and red royal icing on the airplane shapes to represent lights and windows.

FOR THE TOY BOX FRONT:

1. Roll out a 1-oz. piece of blue fondant to about $^1/_{16}$" thick. Cut out a capital T, O, Y, and S with letter cutters and attach them to the front piece with a small dab of water.

Assemble the boxes

(Reference: The Basics of Construction, pages 42–45)

1. With a #3 tip, pipe a strip of brown royal icing on the back edge of a side piece. Attach the front piece to it and reinforce the seam on the inside with a thick strip of icing. You should be able to let it stand on its own right away (a).

2. Repeat this step until all four "walls" are attached. Make sure the box is constructed so that the edges of the side pieces are showing (this gives the front of the box some added definition).

Don't forget to reinforce the seams on the inside (b and c).

3. Repeat steps 1 and 2 for the other box.

4. Let the walls dry for at least 4 hours.

5. Gently lift the walls onto the base pieces and position them in the center (d).

6. Pipe thick strips of icing along the bottom inside of the boxes to secure the walls to the base pieces.

Attach the lids

1. Pipe thick strips of brown royal icing along the top edge of the backs of the boxes.

2. Attach the lids to the back of the boxes, placing folded-up pieces of plastic wrap underneath to hold the lids open (e). Let set for a few minutes, then pipe an extra line of brown royal icing along the

back where the lids meet the boxes.

3. Let everything dry completely overnight.

DAY 2

Fill the boxes

1. Remove the plastic wrap from underneath the lids of the boxes. The lids should be secure, but it's important to handle the boxes gently.

2. Fill the boxes with cookies—each box should fit about 12.

3. Package or display as desired.

CANDY-FILLED HOUSES

Ever since I was a little girl, I've loved the idea of secret compartments containing hidden treats and treasures. These little houses are inspired by that idea—their roofs, which aren't attached to the walls, can be lifted off to reveal little bags of candy hidden inside. After the treats are removed, the lid can be replaced and the house displayed—if it isn't eaten first!

Yield: 2 houses
Difficulty Level: 3
Finished Size: About 4½" high

WHAT YOU'LL NEED

RECIPES

- 1 royal icing recipe *(page 31)*
- 1 gingerbread recipe *(page 23)*

TOOLS

- Scissors
- Pencil and eraser
- Ruler
- Cutting mat
- Craft knife
- Glue gun
- Basic baking equipment (stand mixer or sturdy hand mixer, bowls, measuring cups and spoons, sieve, rubber spatula)
- Toothpicks
- Small bowls
- Small spoons
- Airtight plastic containers for storing icing colors

- Rolling pins (large and small)
- ⅛" thickness strips
- Paring knife
- Cookie sheet
- Cooling rack
- Three piping bags and sets of couplers
- Three #1 piping tips
- Ball tool
- Foam flower making mat
- One #3 piping tip
- One #18 star piping tip
- One #10 piping tip

MATERIALS

- Foam core or thick cardboard (for templates)
- Foam core (for presentation boards)
- Thin white ribbon (to trim presentation board and tie candy bags)

- Blue, red, brown, and green food coloring gel
- Parchment paper
- About 3 oz. rolled fondant
- Red and white candy hearts
- Red-and-white-striped mint candies
- Small cellophane bags

CUTTERS

- 1" circle cutter for the door (or you can use the base of a regular piping tip)
- Small flower cutter

TEMPLATES

The templates for this project can be found on page 159.

TECHNIQUES USED

- Making a template *(page 11)*
- Making a presentation board *(page 13)*
- Making royal icing *(page 31)*
- Coloring royal icing *(page 32)*
- Storing royal icing *(page 32)*

- Preparing the dough *(page 22)*
- Rolling and cutting the dough *(pages 24–25)*
- Baking basics *(pages 26–27)*
- Filling a piping bag *(page 33)*
- Piping techniques *(pages 35–36)*

- Flooding an outline *(pages 37–38)*
- Coloring, rolling, and shaping rolled fondant *(pages 40–41)*
- Construction basics *(pages 42–45)*

METHOD

DAY 1

Prepare your templates

(Reference: Making a Template, page 11)

You can use either foam core or thick cardboard to make the templates for this project. The templates can be found on page 159.

Prepare your presentation boards

(Reference: Presentation Boards, page 13)

I recommend that the presentation boards for this project be at least 4" x 5".

Make royal icing

(Reference: Royal Icing, pages 30–33)

1. Make a full recipe of royal icing *(page 31)*.

2. Divide it roughly into four portions; tint one portion light blue, one red, and one brown. Leave the last portion white.

3. Cover each color tightly with plastic wrap or transfer to airtight containers and set aside.

Bake gingerbread pieces

(Reference: Working with Gingerbread, pages 18–27)

1. Make a full recipe of gingerbread dough *(page 23)*.

2. Roll out a sheet of gingerbread between two sheets of parchment paper using ⅛" thickness strips (or if you're not using strips, roll the gingerbread as close as possible to ⅛" thick), and then remove top parchment paper. Then cut shapes. You'll need:

   • **2 front pieces with door cutout** *(see page 91 for instructions on cutting a door)*
   • **2 back pieces**
   • **4 side pieces**
   • **4 roof pieces**

3. Bake according to the guidelines on pages 26–27.

4. Let the pieces cool completely.

5. Repeat steps 2 through 4 until all the pieces are baked.

Prepare your piping bags

(Reference: Filling a Piping Bag, page 33)

1. Prepare three piping bags with couplers and #1 tips.

2. Fill one of the piping bags with white royal icing, one with red royal icing, and one with light blue royal icing, reserving about half of the white and light blue. Make sure to cover reserved and unused portions when not in use.

Outline and flood the roof shapes

(Reference: Piping Techniques, pages 35–36; Flooding an Outline, pages 37–38)

1. Pipe outlines around two of the roof shapes with white royal icing.

2. Pipe outlines around two of the roof shapes with blue royal icing.

3. Thin the reserved portions of white and light blue royal icing with small amounts of water (no more than one teaspoon at a time) until you reach the desired flooding consistency.

4. Flood all the roof shapes with their corresponding colors. Set aside and let dry for about two hours.

Decorate the shapes

(Reference: Piping Techniques, pages 35–36; Rolled Fondant, pages 40–41)

Using the illustrations on the following page, and photos as a guide, decorate the house shapes as follows:

HOUSE #1

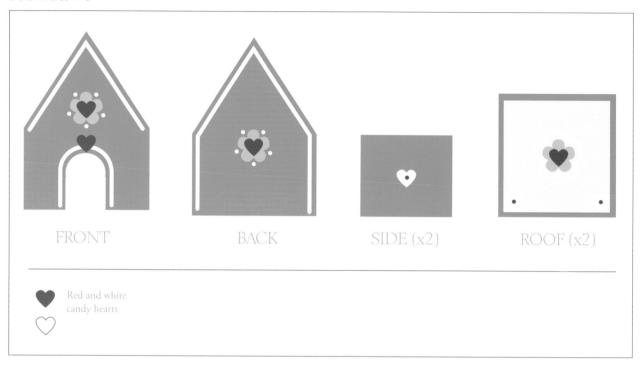

FRONT   BACK   SIDE (x2)   ROOF (x2)

♥ Red and white candy hearts

♡

HOUSE #2

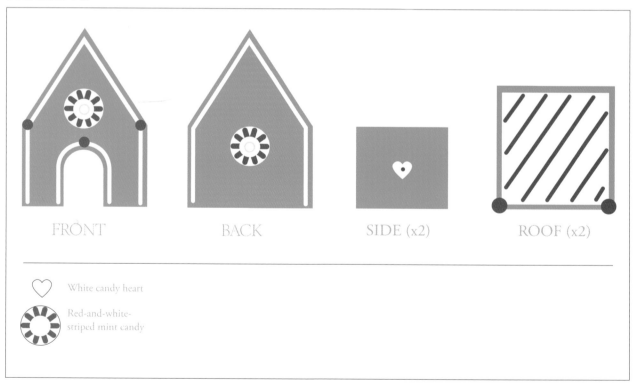

FRONT   BACK   SIDE (x2)   ROOF (x2)

♡ White candy heart

Red-and-white-striped mint candy

This diagram shows how the individual pieces should look before the houses are assembled. Use it as a guide for piping lines and dots, and for placing candies.

FOR HOUSE #1:

1. Tint a 1-oz. piece of fondant light green and roll out to about 1/16" thick. Cut out four small flower shapes and indent the petals with a ball tool (see page 41). Attach to the roof, front, and back pieces with a dot of royal icing.

2. Attach heart-shaped candies to the front, back, side, and roof pieces with a small dot of royal icing.

3. Pipe dots and lines to complete the details.

FOR HOUSE #2:

1. Pipe dots and lines on the roof, front, and back pieces.

2. Attach mint candies to the front and back pieces with royal icing, and heart-shaped candies to the sides.

3. Pipe dots to complete the details.

4. Tint a 1-oz. piece of rolled fondant red (or use pre-tinted as red can be difficult to tint). Roll small balls of red fondant and attach to the bottom corners of the roof pieces with a dot of royal icing. Wrap the leftover red fondant for later use.

5. Let all pieces dry completely overnight.

DAY 2

For the walls, these houses follow the same general construction steps as most houses (see pages 42–45 for a step-by-step description, with photos, of basic house construction). Remember that because they're removable, the roofs are constructed differently— detailed instructions are below, and their corresponding photos are provided on the next page.

Build the walls

(Reference: The Basics of Construction, pages 42–45)

1. Prepare a piping bag with a coupler and a #3 tip and fill with brown royal icing.

2. Pipe a strip of icing on the back edge of a front piece.

3. Stand the front piece up and attach the corresponding side piece to it. You should be able to let it stand on its own right away.

4. Pipe a strip of icing along the side edge of the second side panel and attach it to the other side of the front panel.

5. Pipe a strip of icing along both inside edges of the back panel and attach them to the side panels (a).

6. Reinforce the seams by piping thick strips of icing on the inside.

7. Repeat steps 1 through 6 for the other house.

8. Let the houses dry for at least 6 hours.

Assemble the roofs

This part can be a bit tricky to do by yourself. If possible, enlist a helper! Remember, unlike regular houses, when you assemble these roofs you're omitting the step of piping strips of icing along the top edges of the front and back roof panels.

1. Pipe a thick strip of brown royal icing along the edge of one of the roof pieces.

2. Carefully place the roof pieces together on top of the house so that the strip of icing on the first roof piece meets the edge of the other roof piece (b).

3. Ask a helper to pipe another strip on top of the roof to reinforce it.

4. Since the roof doesn't have any extra icing support underneath, you'll need to hold it in place for about 15 minutes—longer than you normally would have to.

5. After 15 minutes, gently remove your hands, taking care not to shift the roof pieces.

6. Repeat steps 1 through 5 for the other house and let all pieces dry completely overnight.

DAY 3

Reinforce the roofs

1. Carefully lift the roof off the house, turn over, and place gently down on your work surface.

2. Pipe a thick strip of brown royal icing along the inside roof seam—this will give it added reinforcement. Be careful to leave at least ½" on either side though, so the icing doesn't touch the walls when the roof is replaced (c).

3. Carefully replace the roof.

4. Repeat steps 1 through 3 for the other house.

Prepare your treats for the inside

You can fill these little houses with anything you want—I filled mine with the same mints that I used to decorate them. Package them up in clear plastic treat bags tied with a ribbon.

Finish the houses

(Reference: Piping Techniques, pages 35–36; Rolled Fondant, pages 40–41)

FOR HOUSE #1:

1. Lift the house (holding it by the body of the house, not the roof) onto your presentation board and position it as desired.

2. With a piping bag fitted with a #18 (star) tip and filled with very thick white royal icing, pipe a shell border along the top of the roof seam (d).

3. Switch the tip to a #10 round tip and pipe "snow" around the base to secure the house to the presentation board (e).

4. Attach two mint candies at the front of the house on either side.

5. Let dry overnight. Once everything is completely dry, remove the roof and place the candy bags inside.

6. Package or display as desired.

FOR HOUSE #2:

1. Lift the house (holding it by the body of the house, not the roof) onto your presentation board and position it as desired.

2. Make a double rolled rope with white and red fondant *(see rope instructions on page 41)*, and attach along the roof seam with a small amount of brown royal icing. Trim off ends on either side with a sharp craft knife.

3. With a piping bag fitted with a #10 round tip, pipe "snow" around the base to secure the house to the presentation board.

4. Let dry overnight. Once everything is completely dry, remove the roof and place the candy bags inside.

5. Package or display as desired.

CLASSIC CANDY HOUSE

As a child, my favorite fairy tale was always Hansel and Gretel. The witch didn't bother me—all I cared about was imagining the candy house and how much fun it would be to break chunks of it off and eat to my heart's content. This house is a manifestation of that fantasy! It's a perfect project to work on with children; the piping is simple and showcases the rainbow of colors on this candy-studded fantasy home.

Yield: 1 house
Difficulty Level: 2
Finished Size: About 8" high

RECIPES

- 1 royal icing recipe (page 31)
- 1 gingerbread recipe (page 23)

TOOLS

- Scissors
- Pencil and eraser
- Ruler
- Cutting mat
- Craft knife
- Glue gun
- Basic baking equipment (stand mixer or sturdy hand mixer, bowls, measuring cups and spoons, sieve, rubber spatula)
- Toothpicks
- Small bowls
- Small spoons
- Airtight plastic containers for storing icing colors

- Rolling pin (large)
- 1/8" thickness strips
- Paring knife
- Cookie sheet
- Cooling rack
- Two piping bags and sets of couplers
- One #2 piping tip
- One #4 piping tip
- One #10 piping tip

MATERIALS

- Foam core or thick cardboard (for templates)
- Foam core (for presentation board)
- Ribbon to trim presentation board
- Brown food coloring gel
- Parchment paper
- Red-and-white-striped mint candies

- Assorted colors of jelly beans
- Assorted colors of gumdrops
- Candy-coated chocolate pieces
- Candy "lime" slices
- Candy canes

CUTTERS

- 1½" circle cutter (window)
- 2¼" circle cuttter (door)

TEMPLATES

The templates for this project can be found on pages 160–161.

TECHNIQUES USED

- Making a template (page 11)
- Making a presentation board (page 13)
- Making royal icing (page 31)
- Coloring royal icing (page 32)

- Storing royal icing (page 32)
- Preparing the dough (page 22)
- Rolling and cutting the dough (pages 24–25)
- Baking basics (pages 26–27)

- Filling a piping bag (page 33)
- Piping techniques (pages 35–36)
- Construction basics (pages 42–45)

METHOD

DAY 1

Prepare your templates

(Reference: Making a Template, page 11)

You can use either foam core or thick cardboard to make the templates for this project. The templates can be found on pages 160–161.

Prepare your presentation board

(Reference: Presentation Boards, page 13)

I recommend that the presentation board for this project be at least 7½" x 7½" square or 9" round.

Make royal icing

(Reference: Royal Icing, pages 30–33)

1. Make a full recipe of royal icing *(page 31)*.

2. Divide it roughly in half; tint one portion brown and leave the other one white.

3. Cover each color tightly with plastic wrap or transfer to airtight containers and set aside.

Bake gingerbread pieces

(Reference: Working with Gingerbread, pages 18–27)

1. Make a full recipe of gingerbread dough *(page 23)*.

2. Roll out a sheet of gingerbread between two sheets of parchment paper using ⅛" thickness strips (or if you're not using strips, roll the gingerbread as close as possible to ⅛" thick), and then remove top parchment paper. Then cut shapes. You'll need:

   - **1 front piece with door cutout** *(see instructions for cutting a door on page 91)* **and window cutout**
   - **1 back piece**
   - **2 side pieces**
   - **2 roof pieces**
   - **1 door piece** *(see instructions on page 91)*

3. Bake according to the guidelines on pages 26–27.

4. Let the pieces cool completely.

5. Repeat steps 2 through 4 until all the pieces are baked.

Prepare your piping bags

(Reference: Royal Icing, pages 30–33)

1. Prepare a piping bag with a coupler and a #2 tip, and fill with white royal icing.

2. Prepare a piping bag with a coupler and a #4 tip and fill with brown royal icing.

Decorate the shapes

(Reference: Piping Techniques, pages 35–36)

1. Using the illustrations on the next page, and photos as a guide, pipe the lines and dots on each of the shapes with white royal icing. Add the candies with a dot of brown royal icing (except for those that are attached along the side edges and the roof seam). Let all the pieces dry for at least 4 hours.

DAY 2

Build and decorate the house

(Reference: The Basics of Construction, pages 42–45; Piping Techniques, pages 35–36)

1. Follow the steps on pages 43–45 (Building a Simple House) to construct the house. Let it dry as directed and transfer it to your presentation board. Add the door per the instructions on page 45.

2. With a paring knife, cut two candy canes a little bit shorter than the length of the front edges of the house. Attach them to the sides with royal icing, then attach two candy-coated chocolates to the tops of the canes.

3. Attach lime slices to the top of the roof. Slice off the bottom of a red gumdrop with a craft knife and attach to the peak of the roof at the front.

4. With a piping bag fitted with a #10 tip, pipe white royal icing around the base and along the edges of the roof to resemble snow *(see page 36)*.

5. Cut red, white, and green gumdrops and jellybeans in half and stack with mint candies in varying combinations, using white royal icing to attach each piece, to create trees. Arrange the trees around the front and sides of the house and attach each to the board with a bit of icing.

FRONT   BACK   ROOF (x2)   SIDE (x2)   DOOR

Jellybeans

Jellybeans cut in half widthwise

Candy-coated chocolate

Cut-off gumdrops

Red-and-white-striped mint candies

Candy "lime" slices

This diagram shows how the individual pieces should look before the house is assembled. Use it as a guide for piping lines and dots, and for placing candies.

MAKING A DOORWAY CUTOUT AND A DOOR SHAPE:

There's no need to cut a template for making doors. All you need to make a perfectly rounded doorway and its corresponding door is a circle cutter and a paring knife.

1.
Press a circle cutter in the middle of the front piece and cut lines on either side down to the bottom with a paring knife, using a ruler as a guide.

2.
Remove the inside pieces and bake the front piece according to the guidelines on pages 26–27.

1.
On a separate piece of ginger-bread, make a half circle cut by pressing down only the top half of a circle cutter.

2.
Cut lines on either side of the half circle and across the bottom, creating a door shape, using a ruler as a guide.

3.
Remove the excess dough from around the door and bake according to the guidelines on pages 26–27.

LOVE SHACK

Mmm . . . chocolate. Dark chocolate, milk chocolate, and everything in between—I love it all. This house, inspired by a luscious box of gourmet chocolates, makes a perfect gift for a loved one, on Valentine's Day or any other day of the year. Made with delicious chocolate gingerbread, it's covered with mini heart-shaped cookies decorated like chocolate truffles. I guess it's true what they say—home really is where the heart is!

Yield: 1 house
Difficulty Level: 2
Finished Size: About 8" high

WHAT YOU'LL NEED

RECIPES

- 1 royal icing recipe *(page 31)*
- 1 chocolate gingerbread recipe *(page 23)*

TOOLS

- Scissors
- Pencil and eraser
- Ruler
- Cutting mat
- Craft knife
- Glue gun
- Basic baking equipment (stand mixer or sturdy hand mixer, bowls, measuring cups and spoons, sieve, rubber spatula)
- Toothpicks
- Small bowls
- Small spoons

- Airtight plastic containers for storing icing colors
- Rolling pins (large and small)
- ⅛" thickness strips
- Paring knife
- Cookie sheet
- Cooling rack
- Three piping bags and sets of couplers
- Three #1 piping tips
- One #4 piping tip
- One #10 piping tip

MATERIALS

- Foam core or thick cardboard (for templates)
- Foam core (for presentation board)
- Ribbon to trim presentation board
- Pink and brown food coloring gel

- Parchment paper
- About 2 oz. rolled fondant

CUTTERS

- Small heart cutter (1½")
- Large heart cutter (2")
- 1½" circle cutter (for door)

TEMPLATES

The templates for this project can be found on pages 160–161.

TECHNIQUES USED

- Making a template *(page 11)*
- Making a presentation board *(page 13)*
- Making royal icing *(page 31)*
- Coloring royal icing *(page 32)*
- Storing royal icing *(page 32)*

- Preparing the dough *(page 22)*
- Rolling and cutting the dough *(pages 24–25)*
- Baking basics *(pages 26–27)*
- Filling a piping bag *(page 33)*
- Piping techniques *(pages 35–36)*

- Flooding an outline *(pages 37–38)*
- Construction basics *(pages 42–45)*
- Coloring, rolling, and shaping rolled fondant *(pages 40–41)*

METHOD

DAY 1

Prepare your templates

(Reference: Making a Template, page 11)

You can use either foam core or thick cardboard to make the templates for this project. The templates can be found on pages 160–161.

Prepare your presentation board

(Reference: Presentation Boards, page 13)

I recommend that the presentation board for this project be at least 7½" x 7½" square or 9" round.

Make royal icing

(Reference: Royal Icing, pages 30–33)

1. Make a full recipe of royal icing *(page 31)*.

2. Divide it roughly in half; tint one half light pink. Divide the other half in half again; tint half brown and leave the other half white.

3. Cover each color tightly with plastic wrap or transfer to airtight containers and set aside.

Bake gingerbread pieces

(Reference: Working with Gingerbread, pages 18–27)

1. Make a full recipe of chocolate gingerbread dough *(page 23)*.

2. Roll out a sheet of gingerbread between two sheets of parchment paper using ⅛" thickness strips (or if you're not using strips, roll the gingerbread as close as possible to ⅛" thick), and then remove top parchment paper. Then cut shapes. You'll need:

- **1 front piece with door cutout** *(see page 91 for instructions on cutting a door)* **and a 1½" heart shaped window cutout**
- **1 back piece**
- **2 side pieces**
- **2 roof pieces**
- **1 door piece**
- **8 small heart shapes**
- **8 large heart shapes**

3. Bake according to the guidelines on pages 26–27.

4. Let the pieces cool completely.

5. Repeat steps 2 through 4 until all the pieces are baked.

Prepare your piping bags

(Reference: Filling a Piping Bag, page 33)

1. Prepare three piping bags with couplers and #1 tips.

2. Fill one piping bag with white royal icing, one with brown royal icing, and one with light pink royal icing, reserving at least half of the brown and pink.

Outline and flood the shapes

(Reference: Piping Techniques, pages 35–36; Flooding an Outline, pages 37–38)

1. Pipe outlines around the roof

shapes and the door with light pink royal icing.

2. Pipe outlines around half of the medium heart shapes and half of the mini heart shapes with light pink royal icing.

3. Pipe outlines around half of the medium heart shapes and half of the mini heart shapes with brown royal icing.

4. Thin the reserved portions of light pink and brown royal icing with small amounts of water (no more than one teaspoon at a time) until you reach the desired flooding consistency.

5. Flood all the outlined shapes with their corresponding colors. Set aside and let dry for about two hours.

Decorate the shapes

(Reference: Piping Techniques, pages 35–36)

1. Using the illustrations and photos as a guide, pipe the lines, dots, and hearts on each of the house shapes with white royal icing. Pipe lines, spirals, and hearts on each of the heart-shaped cookies with light pink and brown royal icing.

FRONT   BACK   ROOF (x2)   SIDE (x2)

This diagram shows how the individual pieces should look before the house is assembled. Use it as a guide for piping lines and dots, and for attaching the heart-shaped cookies.

Use this diagram as a guide for piping designs on the individual heart-shaped cookies.

2. Attach two mini heart cookies to the front and back of the house and a large pink heart-shaped cookie to each side piece and each roof piece.

3. Let all the pieces dry completely overnight.

DAY 2

Build and decorate the house

(Reference: The Basics of Construction, pages 42–45; Rolled Fondant, pages 40–41; Piping Techniques, pages 35–36)

1. Follow the steps on pages 43–45 (Building a Simple House) to construct the house. Let it dry as directed and transfer it to your presentation board. Add the door per the instructions on page 45.

2. Tint 1 oz. of rolled fondant light pink and 1 oz. brown (I recommend using pre-tinted brown fondant).

3. Follow the steps on page 41 (Ropes and Twisted Ropes) to make a brown and light pink twisted rope and attach it to the top of the roof using brown royal icing. Trim off the ends.

4. With a piping bag fitted with a #10 tip, pipe white royal icing around the base and along the edges of the roof to resemble snow *(see page 36)*.

5. Add a small heart-shaped cookie to the peak of the roof at the front, and add the remaining cookies around the base of the house.

PIPING A SMALL HEART SHAPE

1.

Using a #1 piping tip, pipe a dot of royal icing, decreasing pressure on the piping bag as you draw the tip downward and to the right to create a point.

2.

Repeat, bringing the point of the second dot downward and to the left to meet the first dot.

BIRDHOUSE

Little fondant flowers in different pastel shades, accented with a bit of color dust, give this sweet little birdhouse a fresh Spring look that's perfect for Easter. Individual roof tiles add to the charm and give it a rustic, country feel. However, it's the two adorable little fondant birds perched on their house that make this project so memorable—and they're incredibly easy to make.

Yield: 1 house
Difficulty Level: 3
Finished Size: About 9" high

WHAT YOU'LL NEED

RECIPES

- 1 royal icing recipe *(page 31)*
- 1 gingerbread recipe *(page 23)*

TOOLS

- Scissors
- Pencil and eraser
- Ruler
- Cutting mat
- Craft knife
- Glue gun
- Basic baking equipment (stand mixer or sturdy hand mixer, bowls, measuring cups and spoons, sieve, rubber spatula)
- Toothpicks
- Small bowls
- Small spoons
- Airtight plastic containers for storing icing colors

- Rolling pins (large and small)
- ⅛" thickness strips
- Paring knife
- Cookie sheet
- Cooling rack
- Three piping bags and sets of couplers
- Two #1 piping tips
- One #4 piping tip
- Ball tool
- Foam flower making mat
- Small paintbrush
- One #10 piping tip

MATERIALS

- Foam core or thick cardboard (for templates)
- Foam core (for presentation board)
- Ribbon to trim presentation board

- Yellow, brown, blue, green, pink, and orange food coloring gel
- Parchment paper
- About 6 oz. rolled fondant
- Pink, green, and blue edible dust colors

CUTTERS

- 1½" circle cutter
- 3" flower cutter
- ½" flower cutter
- ¾" flower cutter
- Small leaf cutter (about ⅝" long)

TEMPLATES

The templates for this project can be found on pages 162–163.

TECHNIQUES USED

- Making a template *(page 11)*
- Making a presentation board *(page 13)*
- Making royal icing *(page 31)*
- Coloring royal icing *(page 32)*
- Storing royal icing *(page 32)*

- Preparing the dough *(page 22)*
- Rolling and cutting the dough *(pages 24–25)*
- Baking basics *(pages 26–27)*
- Filling a piping bag *(page 33)*
- Piping techniques *(pages 35–36)*

- Flooding an outline *(pages 37–38)*
- Coloring, rolling, and shaping rolled fondant *(pages 40–41)*
- Adding color dust *(page 103)*
- Construction basics *(pages 42–45)*

METHOD

DAY 1

Prepare your templates

(Reference: Making a Template, page 11)

You can use either foam core or thick cardboard to make the templates for this project. The templates can be found on pages 162–163.

Prepare your presentation board

(Reference: Presentation Boards, page 13)

I recommend that the presentation board for this project be at least 8" x 8" square or 9" round.

Make royal icing

(Reference: Royal Icing, pages 30–33)

1. Make a full recipe of royal icing *(page 31)*.

2. Divide it roughly in half; tint one half very light yellow. Divide the other half in half again; tint half brown and leave the other half white.

3. Cover each color tightly with plastic wrap or transfer to air-tight containers and set aside.

Bake gingerbread pieces

(Reference: Working with Gingerbread, pages 18–27)

Be sure to read the baking instructions carefully for this project—unlike most of the others, it includes the extra steps of freezing some of the cut shapes (the roof tiles and some of the flower shapes) and separating them on the baking sheet before baking.

1. Make a full recipe of gingerbread dough *(page 23)*.

2. Roll out a sheet of gingerbread between two sheets of parchment paper using ⅛" thickness strips (or if you're not using strips, roll the gingerbread as close as possible to ⅛" thick), and then remove top parch-

CUTTING ROOF TILES: This is a quick way to cut individual roof tiles—much quicker than cutting each out separately!

1.

With a paring knife, cut a sheet of gingerbread in strips about 1½" wide, then make perpendicular cuts in varying widths, anywhere from ¾" to 1½". Transfer the parchment paper to a baking sheet and freeze for about 20 minutes.

2.

Using the tip of a paring knife, separate the tiles on the parchment paper. Make sure there's ½" of space between each tile before baking.

ment paper. Then cut shapes. You'll need:

- **1 front piece with round door cutout (1½" circle cutter)**
- **1 back piece**
- **2 side pieces**
- **2 roof pieces**
- **2 large (3") flower pieces with 1½" round hole cutouts, cut in half and separated before baking***
- **1 large (3") flower piece with a 1½" round hole cutout**
- **1 front accent strip**
- **2 side accent strips**
- **About 75 roof tiles** (see instructions for cutting roof tiles on the previous page)

3. Bake according to the guidelines on pages 26–27.

4. Let the pieces cool completely.

5. Repeat steps 2 through 4 until all the pieces are baked.

Prepare your piping bags

(Reference: Filling a Piping Bag, page 33)

1. Prepare two piping bags with couplers and #1 tips and fill one with light yellow royal icing, reserving about ⅔ of it, and fill the other bag with white royal icing.

2. Prepare a piping bag with couplers and a #4 tip and fill with brown royal icing.

Outline and flood the shapes

(Reference: Piping Techniques, pages 35–36; Flooding an Outline, pages 37–38)

1. Pipe outlines around the front, back, and side shapes with light yellow royal icing.

2. Thin the reserved portion of light yellow icing with small amounts of water (no more than one teaspoon at a time) until you reach the desired flooding consistency.

3. Flood all the outlined shapes with the yellow icing. Set aside and let dry for about two hours.

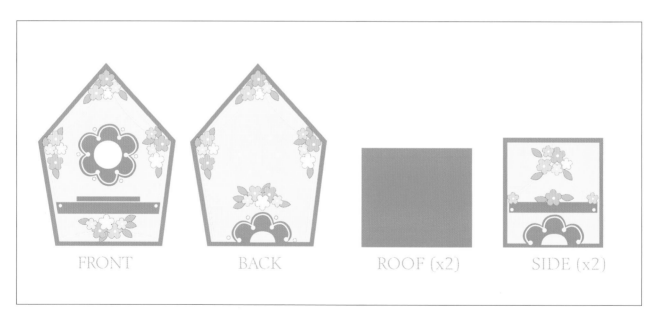

FRONT   BACK   ROOF (x2)   SIDE (x2)

This diagram shows how the individual pieces should look before the house is assembled. Use it as a guide for piping lines and dots, and for placing the fondant flowers.

* Like the roof tiles, the flower halves can be more easily separated by placing the cut shapes in the freezer for a few minutes.

MAKING A FONDANT BIRD: These birds are adorable and really easy to make.

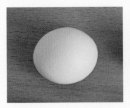    

1.
Tint a 1-oz. piece of fondant light blue (or any other color you wish). Shape it into a ball.

2.
Roll the ball into a pear shape and form one end into a point. Flatten it slightly and give it a slight upward curl.

3.
On each side, attach a small flattened pear-shaped piece of fondant with a small dab of water.

4.
With a toothpick, make two little dots for the bird's eyes.

5.
Tint a small piece of fondant orange. Form a tiny piece of it into a cone shape and attach to the bird's face with a small dab of water.

ADDING COLOR DUST TO FLOWERS: Adding
a little bit of color dust really brings out the beauty of little fondant flowers. Just dip a small paintbrush in the dust, tap off the excess and brush the dust onto the flower, then add a dot in the middle with royal icing.

While the shapes dry, make the fondant birds, flowers, and leaves

(Reference: Rolled Fondant, pages 40–41, and photos on previous page)

1. Tint 2 oz. of rolled fondant light green, 2 oz. light blue, ½ oz. light yellow, ½ oz. light pink, and ½ oz. light orange.

2. Make about 6 small and 6 large flowers with each color of fondant except light green *(see instructions on page 41)*. Let dry for about a ½ hour then add color dust *(see previous page)* and pipe a dot in the center of each with white royal icing, using a #1 piping tip. Set aside to dry.

3. Make about 40 leaves. To make leaves, roll a small amount of fondant into a sheet about ⅛" thick. Cut a leaf shape and remove excess. Transfer the leaf onto a foam flower making mat and press a ball tool around the edges of the leaf to thin them. Pinch the bottom of the leaf together. Let dry for about a ½ hour.

4. Make the fondant birds *(see previous page for instructions)*. Set aside to dry.

Decorate the shapes

(Reference: Piping Techniques, pages 35–36)

1. Using the illustrations on page 102, and photos as a guide, attach the flower piece (with the hole cutout) over the hole in the front of the house with light yellow royal icing. Attach the half flower pieces with hole cutouts to the sides and back.

2. Attach the accent strips to the front and sides of the house with light yellow royal icing.

3. Pipe a strip of light yellow royal icing along the long edge of the half flower piece and attach to the front of the house, against the accent strip, so that it's standing straight up (this creates the ledge that the bird sits on).

4. Attach one bird to the top of the house and one to the ledge using white royal icing, so that it looks like they're sitting in the snow.

5. Using the illustrations and photos as a guide, pipe dots and lines on the front, back, and side pieces with light yellow royal icing.

6. Attach the fondant flowers and leaves to the front, back, and side pieces with a dot of yellow royal icing.

7. Let all the pieces dry completely overnight.

DAY 2

Build and decorate the house

(Reference: The Basics of Construction, pages 42–45; Piping Techniques, pages 35–36)

TRY THIS!

When you're baking the roof tiles, leave some in the oven longer than others. When you attach them to the roof, alternate the darker ones with the lighter ones to create a variegated effect.

1. Follow the steps on pages 43–45 (Building a Simple House) to construct the house. (The edges of the front and back pieces are slightly angled for this house, so make sure to align the sides accordingly.) Let it dry as directed and transfer it to your presentation board.

2. Attach the roof tiles using a large dot of brown royal icing for each one, starting at the bottom and moving upward, and alternating wide and narrow tiles *(see photo below)*. Let the tiles dry for about an hour.

3. With a piping bag fitted with a #10 tip, pipe white royal icing around the base and along the edges of the roof to resemble snow *(see page 36)*.

4. Attach one bird to the top of the house and one to the ledge using white royal icing, so that it looks like they're sitting in the snow.

GARDEN COTTAGE

Gingerbread houses don't always have to be covered in snow! This little cottage, covered in lush vines and surrounded by greenery, looks like the perfect summer hideaway.

With this project there are so many possibilities for color combinations. Changing the color of the roof, door, and flowers of this house would give it a completely different look, so feel free to experiment!

Yield: 1 house
Difficulty Level: 3
Finished Size: About 8" high

WHAT YOU'LL NEED

RECIPES

- 1 royal icing recipe *(page 31)*
- 1 gingerbread recipe *(page 23)*

TOOLS

- Scissors
- Pencil and eraser
- Ruler
- Cutting mat
- Craft knife
- Glue gun
- Basic baking equipment (stand mixer or sturdy hand mixer, bowls, measuring cups and spoons, sieve, rubber spatula)
- Toothpicks
- Small bowls
- Small spoons

- Airtight plastic containers for storing icing colors
- Rolling pins (large and small)
- ⅛" thickness strips
- Paring knife
- Cookie sheet
- Cooling rack
- Four piping bags and sets of couplers
- Two #1 piping tips
- Ball tool
- Foam flower making mat
- One # 2 piping tip
- One #4 piping tip
- One #67 leaf piping tip

MATERIALS

- Foam core or thick cardboard (for templates)
- Foam core (for presentation board)

- Ribbon to trim presentation board
- Blue, green, brown, yellow, and pink food coloring gel
- Parchment paper
- About 2 oz. rolled fondant
- 2 cups crushed cornflakes cereal

CUTTERS

- 2¼" circle cutter (door)
- Small flower cutter

TEMPLATES

The templates for this project can be found on pages 160–161.

TECHNIQUES USED

- Making a template *(page 11)*
- Making a presentation board *(page 13)*
- Making royal icing *(page 31)*
- Coloring royal icing *(page 32)*
- Storing royal icing *(page 32)*

- Preparing the dough *(page 22)*
- Rolling and cutting the dough *(pages 24–25)*
- Baking basics *(pages 26–27)*
- Filling a piping bag *(page 33)*
- Piping techniques *(pages 35–36)*

- Flooding an outline *(pages 37–38)*
- Coloring, rolling, and shaping rolled fondant *(pages 40–41)*
- Construction basics *(pages 42–45)*

METHOD

DAY 1

Prepare your templates

(Reference: Making a Template, page 11)

You can use either foam core or thick cardboard to make most of the templates for this project. For the flower box templates, I recommend using a thinner material, such as a heavy cardstock. The templates can be found on pages 160–161.

Prepare your presentation board

(Reference: Presentation Boards, page 13)

I recommend that the presentation board for this project be at least 7½" x 7½" square or 9" round.

Make royal icing

(Reference: Royal Icing, pages 30–33)

1. Make a full recipe of royal icing *(page 31)*.

2. Divide it roughly into three portions; tint one portion blue and one portion green. Divide the last portion in half; tint one half brown and the other half very light yellow.

3. Cover each color tightly with plastic wrap or transfer to air-tight containers and set aside.

Bake gingerbread pieces

(Reference: Working with Gingerbread, pages 18–27)

1. Make a full recipe of ginger-bread dough *(page 23)*.

2. Roll out a sheet of gingerbread between two sheets of parchment paper using ⅛" thickness strips (or if you're not using strips, roll the gingerbread as close as possible to ⅛" thick), and then remove top parchment paper. Then cut shapes. You'll need:

   - **1 front piece with door cutout**
     (see page 91 for instructions on cutting a door)
   - **1 back piece**
   - **2 side pieces**
   - **2 roof pieces**
   - **1 door piece**
     (see instructions on page 91)
   - **3 flower box front pieces**
   - **3 flower box bottom pieces**
   - **6 flower box side pieces**
   - **4 shutter pieces**

3. Bake according to the guide-lines on pages 26–27.

4. Let the pieces cool completely.

5. Repeat steps 2 through 4 until all the pieces are baked.

Prepare your piping bags

(Reference: Filling a Piping Bag, page 33)

1. Prepare a piping bag with a coupler and a #1 tip and fill with blue royal icing, reserving about ⅔ of it.

2. Prepare a piping bag with a cou-pler and a #1 tip and fill with light yellow royal icing, reserving about ½ of it.

Outline and flood the shapes

(Reference: Piping Techniques, pages 35–36; Flooding an Outline, pages 37–38)

1. Pipe outlines around the roof shapes and the door with blue royal icing.

2. Pipe outlines around the top part of the front and back shapes with light yellow royal icing.

3. Thin the reserved portions of blue and light yellow royal icing with small amounts of water (no more than one teaspoon at a time) until you reach the desired flooding consistency.

4. Flood all the outlined shapes with their corresponding colors. Set aside and let dry for about two hours.

While the shapes dry, make the fondant flowers

(Reference: Rolled Fondant, pages 40–41)

1. Tint 2 oz. of rolled fondant pink.

2. Make about 30 small flowers *(see page 41 for instructions on making flowers)*. Pipe a dot in the center of each with light yellow royal icing. Set aside to dry.

Decorate the shapes

(Reference: Piping Techniques, pages 35–36)

1. Using the illustrations and photos as a guide, pipe lines and dots on each of the shapes with blue and light yellow royal icing. Set aside to dry for about an hour.

Assemble the flower boxes

1. Using the photos on the opposite page for reference, assemble the flower boxes.

2. Let dry for about two hours.

Attach the window boxes and shutters

1. Prepare a piping bag with a coupler and a #4 tip and fill with brown royal icing.

2. Pipe a strip of icing on the back edges of the flower boxes and attach to the front and side pieces. The side flower boxes should go right under the window and the front box should go in the middle of the yellow flooded area.

3. Reinforce the flower boxes by piping a thick strip of royal icing along the inside edges of the boxes (this won't be visible after the greenery has been added).

4. Let all pieces dry completely overnight.

DAY 2

Build the house

(Reference: The Basics of Construction, pages 42–45)

HELPFUL TIP

The flower boxes add some extra weight to the walls of the house. When you're assembling the house, you may have to hold the walls in place for a little longer.

1. Follow the steps on pages 43–45 (Building a Simple House) to construct the house. Let it dry as directed and transfer it to your presentation board. Add the door per the instructions on page 45.

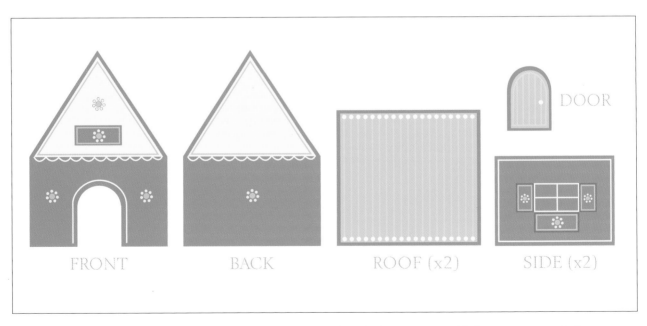

This diagram shows how the individual pieces should look before the house is assembled. Use it as a guide for piping lines and dots, and placing the flower boxes and shutters.

Add the vines, greenery, and flowers

(Reference: Piping Techniques, pages 35–36, and photos on page 106 and below)

1. With a piping bag fitted with a #4 tip, pipe green royal icing along the base of the house at the corners (this will help adhere the house to the presentation board, and will be covered by the "bushes").

2. Combine 2 cups of crushed cornflakes and ½ cup of green royal icing (a).

3. Shape into small bunches and place along the bottom of the house and inside the flower boxes, securing with green royal icing at the bottom (b).

4. Change the piping bag with green icing to a #67 leaf tip and pipe leaves along the edges of the roof, the sides of the house, and around the door, to resemble vines. Make sure the icing you use for the leaves is thick enough to hold the shape of the leaf—if necessary, thicken with icing sugar.

5. Attach the pink flowers where desired with a dot of green royal icing.

a.

b.

MAKING THE FLOWER BOXES:

1.
Using a piping bag fitted with a #2 tip, pipe a strip of brown royal icing along the front edge of the bottom piece and attach the front piece to it.

2.
Pipe a strip of royal icing along the bottom and front edge of a side piece and attach it as shown above.

3.
Attach the other side piece the same way.

4.
When all the pieces are attached, pipe reinforcing strips of royal icing along the inside edges of the flower box. Let dry for about 2 hours.

ICE-CREAM PARLOR

Dripping with chocolate and topped with "whipped cream," sprinkles, and a gumdrop cherry, this house makes me happy—and has me craving an ice-cream sundae every time I look at it. This project is a lot of fun to make—you'll hand-dip the sugar cone trees and actually pour melted chocolate over the house—the drippier, the better!

Yield: 1 house
Difficulty Level: 3
Finished Size: About 8" high

WHAT YOU'LL NEED

RECIPES

- 1 royal icing recipe *(page 31)*
- 1 gingerbread recipe *(page 23)*

TOOLS

- Scissors
- Pencil and eraser
- Ruler
- Cutting mat
- Craft knife
- Glue gun
- Basic baking equipment (stand mixer or sturdy hand mixer, bowls, measuring cups and spoons, sieve, rubber spatula)
- Toothpicks
- Small bowls
- Small spoons
- Airtight plastic containers for storing icing colors
- Rolling pins (large and small)
- ⅛" thickness strips
- Paring knife
- Cookie sheet
- Cooling rack
- Three piping bags and sets of couplers
- Three #1 piping tips
- One #4 piping tip
- Large serrated-edge knife
- One #10 piping tip
- One #18 star piping tip

MATERIALS

- Foam core or thick cardboard (for templates)
- Foam core (for presentation board)
- Ribbon to trim presentation board
- Pink, brown, and yellow food coloring gel
- Parchment paper
- About 6 oz. rolled fondant
- 1½ cups chocolate candy wafers
- Vegetable oil
- 6 to 8 sugar cones
- Multicolored sprinkles
- Wax paper
- 4 large red gumdrops
- 2 small red round gumdrops

CUTTERS

- 1½" circle cutter (for door and window tops)
- 1" circle cutter (for window and shutters)

TEMPLATES

The templates for this project can be found on pages 160–161.

TECHNIQUES USED

- Making a template *(page 11)*
- Making a presentation board *(page 13)*
- Making royal icing *(page 31)*
- Coloring royal icing *(page 32)*
- Storing royal icing *(page 32)*
- Preparing the dough *(page 22)*
- Rolling and cutting the dough *(pages 24–25)*
- Baking basics *(pages 26–27)*
- Filling a piping bag *(page 33)*
- Piping techniques *(pages 35–36)*
- Flooding an outline *(pages 37–38)*
- Coloring, rolling, and shaping rolled fondant *(pages 40–41)*
- Construction basics *(pages 42–45)*

METHOD

DAY 1

Prepare your templates

(Reference: Making a Template, page 11)

You can use either foam core or thick cardboard to make the templates for this project. The templates can be found on pages 160–161.

Prepare your presentation board

(Reference: Presentation Boards, page 13)

I recommend that the presentation board for this project be at least 7½" x 7½" square or 9" round.

Make royal icing

(Reference: Royal Icing, pages 30–33)

1. Make a full recipe of royal icing *(page 31)*.

2. Divide it roughly in half; tint one half pink. Divide the remaining half into three portions; tint one portion brown, one portion very light yellow, and leave the last portion white.

3. Cover each color tightly with plastic wrap or transfer to air-tight containers and set aside.

Bake gingerbread pieces

(Reference: Working with Gingerbread, pages 18–27)

1. Make a full recipe of gingerbread dough *(page 23)*.

2. Roll out a sheet of gingerbread between two sheets of parchment paper using ⅛" thickness strips (or if you're not using strips, roll the gingerbread as close as possible to ⅛" thick), and then remove top parchment paper. Then cut shapes. You'll need:

   - **1 front piece with door cutout** *(see instructions for cutting a door on page 91)* **and window cutout**
   - **1 back piece**
   - **2 side pieces**
   - **2 roof pieces**
   - **1 door piece** *(see instructions on page 91)*
   - **4 shutter pieces (2 circles cut in half and separated)**
   - **4 rectangular shutters**
   - **2 side window top pieces**

3. Bake according to the guidelines on pages 26–27.

4. Let the pieces cool completely.

5. Repeat steps 2 through 4 until all the pieces are baked.

Prepare your piping bags

(Reference: Filling a Piping Bag, page 33)

1. Prepare a piping bag with couplers and a #1 tip and fill with light pink royal icing, reserving about ⅔ of it.

2. Prepare a piping bag with a coupler and a #1 tip and fill with light yellow royal icing, reserving about ½ of it.

3. Prepare a piping bag with a coupler and a #1 tip and fill with brown royal icing.

Outline and flood the shapes

(Reference: Piping Techniques, pages 35–36; Flooding an Outline, pages 37–38)

1. Pipe outlines around the roof shapes, the rectangular shutters, and the door with light pink royal icing.

2. Pipe outlines around the top part of the front and back shapes, and the window tops, with light yellow royal icing.

3. Thin the reserved portions of light pink and light yellow royal icing with small amounts of water (no more than one teaspoon at a time) until you reach the desired flooding consistency.

4. Flood all the outlined shapes with their corresponding colors. Sprinkle window tops with multicolored sprinkles. Set aside and let dry for about two hours.

Make the fondant decorations

(Reference: Rolled Fondant, page 40–41)

1. Tint 2 oz. rolled fondant light pink.

2. Shape into small balls (make about 12 to 15) and set aside.

(See page 41 for instructions on making balls.)

3. Tint 2 oz. rolled fondant very light yellow.

4. Tint 2 oz. rolled fondant brown, or use pre-tinted brown (I recommend using pre-tinted).

5. Make 4 rolled ropes with the yellow and brown fondant *(see rope instructions on page 41)*. Roll the ropes again to smooth them out, then trim the ends to the same height as the house sides (a).

Make the ice cream cones and trees

1. In a microwave-safe bowl, melt 1½ cups of chocolate candy wafers. Add 3 tbsp of vegetable oil and mix well.

2. With a large serrated-edge knife, cut the bottoms off some of the sugar cones and the tops and bottoms off others to create different sizes of cone "trees."

3. Dip the wide ends of the cones in the melted chocolate and then the sprinkles and set aside to dry on wax paper. Keep the remaining chocolate for the next day.

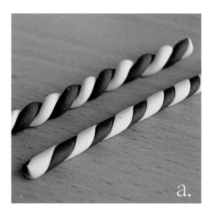
a.

Decorate the shapes

(Reference: Piping Techniques, pages 35–36)

1. Using the illustrations and photos as a guide, pipe dots and lines on each of the shapes with light yellow and brown royal icing. Using a #4 piping tip, attach the shutters and window tops with brown royal icing.

2. Attach the light pink fondant balls to the front piece with either pink or brown royal icing.

3. Attach large cut-off gumdrops to the front and back piece and a small gumdrop to the door.

4. Let all the pieces dry completely overnight.

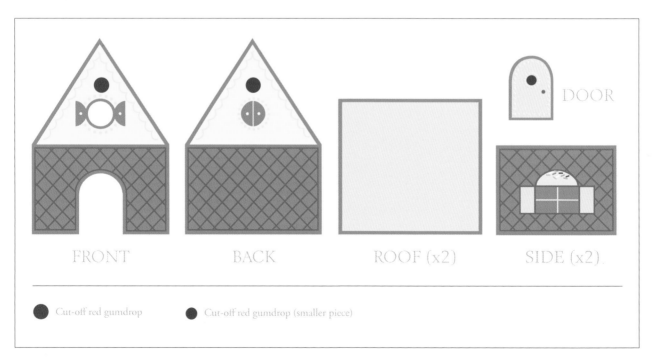

FRONT BACK ROOF (x2) SIDE (x2)

● Cut-off red gumdrop ● Cut-off red gumdrop (smaller piece)

This diagram shows how the individual pieces should look before the house is assembled. Use it as a guide for piping lines and dots, and placing candies.

DAY 2

Build and decorate the house

(Reference: The Basics of Construction, pages 42–45)

1. Follow the steps on pages 43–45 (Building a Simple House) to construct the house. Let it dry as directed and transfer it to your presentation board. Add the door.

Add the remaining details

(Reference: Piping Techniques, pages 35–36)

1. Re-melt the remaining chocolate candy wafers in the microwave. Slowly pour over the top of the house, letting it drip down the sides (b and c). Don't worry if some of the drips land on the presentation board—it only adds to the effect.

2. Let the chocolate cool and set for about 15 minutes.

3. Thin a small amount of the white royal icing slightly, adding water in small amounts. It should be thin enough to pour but not runny.

4. Spoon about 2 tablespoons of the thinned icing on top of the house, pushing it down the sides a bit if necessary to create a runny effect. Sprinkle a few sprinkles on top and attach a large red gumdrop in the middle.

5. With a piping bag fitted with a #10 tip, pipe white royal icing around the base and along the edges of the roof to resemble snow *(see page 36)*— or whipped cream.

6. Place the sugar cone trees around the front and sides of the house, turning the ones with points upside down. With a piping bag fitted with a #18 star tip, pipe swirls of white royal icing in the upright cones to resemble soft-serve ice cream.

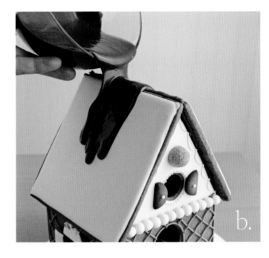

b.

c.

HAUNTED HOUSE

I know haunted houses are supposed to be scary, but I think I'd like to go inside this one; the ghosts are so cute, they couldn't possibly be unfriendly!

Small touches, such as overbaking the shutters and gravestones a little and placing them at an angle, add contrast to the house and give it a weathered look.

Yield: 1 house
Difficulty Level: 3
Finished Size: About 10" high

WHAT YOU'LL NEED

RECIPES

- 1 royal icing recipe *(page 31)*
- 1 gingerbread recipe *(page 23)*

TOOLS

- Scissors
- Pencil and eraser
- Ruler
- Cutting mat
- Craft knife
- Glue gun
- Basic baking equipment (stand mixer or sturdy hand mixer, bowls, measuring cups and spoons, sieve, rubber spatula)
- Toothpicks
- Small bowls
- Small spoons
- Airtight plastic containers for storing icing colors
- Rolling pins (large and small)
- ⅛" thickness strips
- Paring knife
- Cookie sheet
- Cooling rack
- Six piping bags and sets of couplers
- Five #1 piping tips
- Ball tool
- One #2 piping tip
- One #4 piping tip
- One #67 leaf piping tip

MATERIALS

- Foam core or thick cardboard (for templates)
- Foam core (for presentation board)
- Ribbon to trim presentation board
- Purple, brown, black, green, yellow, and orange food coloring gel
- Parchment paper
- About 5 oz. rolled fondant
- Orange and brown candy-coated peanut butter pieces

CUTTERS

- 1" circle cutter (for front window, shutters, and small gravestones)
- 1½" circle cutter (for door, inner window piece, window tops, and large gravestones)
- Small ghost cutter

TEMPLATES

The templates for this project can be found on pages 161, 164–165.

TECHNIQUES USED

- Making a template *(page 11)*
- Making a presentation board *(page 13)*
- Making royal icing *(page 31)*
- Coloring royal icing *(page 32)*
- Storing royal icing *(page 32)*
- Preparing the dough *(page 22)*
- Rolling and cutting the dough *(pages 24–25)*
- Baking basics *(pages 26–27)*
- Filling a piping bag *(page 33)*
- Piping techniques *(pages 35–36)*
- Flooding an outline *(pages 37–38)*
- Coloring, rolling, and shaping rolled fondant *(pages 40–41)*
- Construction basics *(pages 42–45)*

METHOD

DAY 1

Prepare your templates

(Reference: Making a Template, page 11)

You can use either foam core or thick cardboard to make most of the templates for this project. The templates can be found on pages 161, 164–165.

Prepare your presentation board

(Reference: Presentation Boards, page 13)

I recommend that the presentation board for this project be at least 7½" x 7½" square or 9" round.

Make royal icing

(Reference: Royal Icing, pages 30–33)

1. Make a full recipe of royal icing *(page 31)*.

2. Divide it roughly into three portions; tint one portion purple. Divide one of the remaining portions into three parts; tint one brown, one black, and leave the last white. Divide the other remaining portion in half; tint one half green and the other half yellow.

3. Cover each color tightly with plastic wrap or transfer to airtight containers and set aside.

Bake gingerbread pieces

(Reference: Working with Gingerbread, pages 18–27)

1. Make a full recipe of gingerbread dough *(page 23)*.

2. Roll out a sheet of gingerbread between two sheets of parchment paper using ⅛" thickness strips (or if you're not using strips, roll the gingerbread as close as possible to ⅛" thick), and then remove top parchment paper. Then cut shapes. You'll need:

CUTTING RECTANGULAR WINDOWS:
For this house, you'll need to cut rectangular-shaped windows. The easiest way to do this is to place a template on top of the front piece and cut around it, rather than cutting windows into the template and cutting inside them.

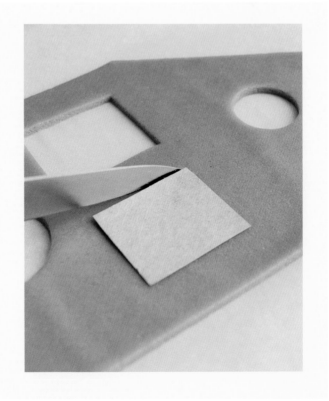

1.
Cut the front piece and add the door and top window cutouts.

2.
Place the window template on the front piece and cut around it, pressing the tip of your paring knife down at each corner. Cut two windows, spacing them apart equally, and remove the excess dough.

- **1 front piece with door cutout** (*see instructions for cutting a door on page 91*) **and window cutouts**
- **1 back piece with window cutouts**
- **2 side pieces with window cutouts**
- **2 roof pieces**
- **1 door piece** (*see instructions on page 91*)
- **12 rectangular shutter pieces**
- **6 rectangular inner window pieces**
- **2 circular inner window pieces (1½" circle cutter)**
- **1 inner door piece**
- **6 window top pieces (1½" circle cut in half and separated)**

- **2 small shutter pieces (1" circle cut in half and separated)**
- **3 mini ghost pieces**
- **2 small gravestone pieces***
- **2 large gravestone pieces***

3. Bake the front, back, side, door, roof, and ghost pieces according to the guidelines on pages 26–27.

4. Overbake the accent pieces (shutters, gravestones, and window tops) a little to give them a darker brown color.

5. Let the pieces cool completely.

6. Repeat steps 2 through 5 until all the pieces are baked.

Prepare your piping bags

(Reference: Filling a Piping Bag, page 33)

1. Prepare three piping bags with couplers and #1 tips. Fill one with purple royal icing, reserving about ⅔ of it. Fill one with white royal icing, reserving about ⅓ of it. And fill the last one with black royal icing.

2. Prepare two piping bags with couplers and a #1 tip and fill one with yellow and one with green royal icing, reserving about ½ of each.

FRONT   BACK   ROOF (x2)   SIDE (x2)

● ● Orange and brown candy-coated peanut butter pieces

This diagram shows how the individual pieces should look before the house is assembled. Use it as a guide for piping lines and dots, and attaching the shutters and window top pieces.

Follow door instructions on page 91 to create the gravestones.

MAKING A FONDANT PUMPKIN: Make a few of these fondant pumpkins to place along the front of the house. They don't have to be perfectly round—some can be short and squat, and some can be long and thin—just like real pumpkins.

1.
Tint 2 oz. of rolled fondant orange. Shape a ½ oz. piece into a ball.

2.
With a ball tool, make a depression in the top of the ball.

3.
Make lines along the sides of the pumpkin with a toothpick.

4.
With a piping bag fitted with a #2 tip, pipe a stem with green royal icing.

Outline and flood the shapes

(Reference: Piping Techniques, pages 35–36; Flooding an Outline, pages 37–38)

1. Pipe outlines around the roof shapes and the door with purple royal icing.

2. Pipe outlines around the top part of the front and back shapes with green royal icing.

3. Pipe outlines around the inner window pieces and the inner door piece with yellow royal icing.

4. Pipe outlines around the miniature ghost pieces with white royal icing.

5. Thin the reserved portions of purple, green, yellow, and white royal icing with small amounts of water (no more than one teaspoon at a time)

until you reach the desired flooding consistency.

6. Flood all the outlined shapes with their corresponding colors and let them dry for about 2 hours.

Decorate the shapes

(Reference: Piping Techniques, pages 35–36)

1. Using the illustrations and photos as a guide, pipe black lines on the yellow window pieces to represent windowpanes, a black outline on the green areas of the front and back pieces, and a black outline around the doorway on the front piece.

2. Pipe a black dot on each of the rectangular shutters.

3. Pipe two small black dots on the ghost pieces for eyes.

4. Pipe white lines on the roof pieces to represent cobwebs and attach a brown candy-coated peanut butter piece to each bottom corner.

5. Attach an orange candy-coated peanut butter piece to the door to represent a doorknob.

6. Let all the pieces dry completely overnight.

DAY 2

Attach the inner window and door pieces

(Reference: Instructions and photos on next page)

Attach the shutters, window top pieces, and ghosts

1. Gently turn the pieces over.

2. Pipe generous dots of brown royal icing on the backs of each shutter and window top and attach to the front of the house, placing them at an angle to give them a "rundown" look.

3. Attach two ghosts to the front piece with brown royal icing.

4. Let all the pieces dry for about 4 hours.

Build the house

(Reference: The Basics of Construction, pages 42–45)

1. Follow the steps on pages 43-45 (Building a Simple House) to construct the house. Let it dry as directed and transfer it to your presentation board. Add the door per the instructions on page 45.

Add the remaining details

(Reference: Piping Techniques, pages 35–36; Rolled Fondant, pages 40–41)

1. Switch the tip of your green piping bag to a #67 leaf tip and pipe some leaves around the bottom edges and a little way up the sides of the house. This will adhere the house to your presentation board.

2. Tint about 3 oz. of rolled fondant brown (or to make it easier, use pre-tinted chocolate fondant) and roll out to about ⅛" thick (you can use your thickness strips for this if you have them). Cut thin strips about ½" wide and the same height as the side piece of the house. Let them dry for about 20 minutes, then attach them to the sides of the house with brown royal icing.

3. Attach the gravestones and orange candy-coated peanut butter pieces to the house with brown royal icing.

ATTACHING THE INNER WINDOWS: To give the windows the appearance of being brightly lit, separate pieces flooded with yellow royal icing are attached on the inside before the house is assembled.

1.

Gently turn the front piece over and lay it flat. Prepare a piping bag with a coupler and a #4 tip and fill with brown royal icing. Lay the inner window and door pieces on top of their corresponding cutouts and pipe outlines around each shape, securing them to the main piece. It's OK if the icing looks a little sloppy—this is all hidden inside the house.

2.

Do the same for the side and back pieces. When all the pieces have dried and you turn them over, they should look like this.

4. Attach the fondant pumpkins around the house with green royal icing.

5. Attach the final ghost piece to the front of the peak of the roof with brown royal icing. You may have to hold it in place for up to 5 minutes.

6. With white royal icing and a #1 tip, pipe a few dangling cobwebs around the front, back, and sides of the roof. To do this, hold the tip of the piping bag against the edge of the roof and pull back slowly while putting pressure on the bag. Release a small stream of icing and then return the tip to the edge of the roof. Pull the piping bag away to cut the stream of icing. Repeat as desired. If a few of the dangling cobwebs break, that's OK—it only adds to the look.

TRY THIS!

For this design, I've used minimal candy, preferring to focus on the contrast of the cobwebs and the ghosts. However, Halloween is all about candy, so feel free to add as much extra candy as you want!

ROCKET

This gingerbread rocket is a blast to make—kids will think it's out of this world! Candy-coated chocolate and gumdrops become twinkling lights and a little fondant alien peeking out of a window adds a cute touch. The rounded top can be intimidating, but baking a curved shape is actually not that difficult. All you need is a small aluminum bowl—available in grocery, dollar, and home stores.

Yield: 1 rocket
Difficulty Level: 4
Finished Size: 12"

RECIPES

- 1 royal icing recipe *(page 31)*
- 1 gingerbread recipe *(page 23)*

TOOLS

- Scissors
- Pencil and eraser
- Ruler
- Cutting mat
- Craft knife
- Glue gun
- Basic baking equipment (stand mixer or sturdy hand mixer, bowls, measuring cups and spoons, sieve, rubber spatula)
- Toothpicks
- Small bowls
- Small spoons
- Airtight plastic containers for storing icing colors

- Rolling pins (large and small)
- ⅛" thickness strips
- ¼" thickness strips
- Paring knife
- Cookie sheet
- Cooling rack
- 5" aluminum mixing bowl
- Three piping bags and sets of couplers
- Two #1 piping tips
- Ball tool
- Small paintbrush
- One #4 piping tip

MATERIALS

- Foam core or thick cardboard (for templates)
- Foam core (for presentation board)
- Ribbon to trim presentation board

- Blue, brown, red, green, and black food coloring gel
- Parchment paper
- Non-stick cooking spray
- About 10 oz. rolled fondant
- Assorted colors of miniature candy-coated chocolate pieces (mostly blue)
- Red gumdrops

CUTTERS

- 1½" circle cutter
- 2¼" circle cutter
- 1¼" circle cutter
- 3" circle cutter

TEMPLATES

The templates for this project can be found on pages 166–167.

- Making a template *(page 11)*
- Making a presentation board *(page 13)*
- Making royal icing *(page 31)*
- Coloring royal icing *(page 32)*
- Storing royal icing *(page 32)*

- Preparing the dough *(page 22)*
- Rolling and cutting the dough *(pages 24–25)*
- Baking basics *(pages 26–27)*
- Filling a piping bag *(page 33)*

- Piping techniques *(pages 35–36)*
- Flooding an outline *(pages 37–38)*
- Coloring, rolling, and shaping rolled fondant *(pages 40–41)*
- Construction basics *(pages 42–45)*

METHOD

DAY 1

Prepare your templates

(Reference: Making a Template, page 11)

You can use either foam core or thick cardboard to make the side panel templates for this project. For the "fin" template, I recommend using a thinner material, such as a heavy cardstock. The templates can be found on pages 166–167.

Prepare your presentation board

(Reference: Presentation Boards, page 13)

I recommend that the presentation board for this project be at least 7" x 7" square or 9" round.

Make royal icing

(Reference: Royal Icing, pages 30–33)

1. Make a full recipe of royal icing *(page 31)*.

2. Divide it roughly in half; tint one half light blue. Divide the other half in half again; tint one brown and the other red.

3. Cover each color tightly with plastic wrap or transfer to airtight containers and set aside.

Bake the ⅛" thick gingerbread pieces

(Reference: Working with Gingerbread, pages 18–27)

Note: For this project, you'll cut some shapes from ⅛" thick dough and some from ¼" thick dough.

BAKING THE ROUNDED CAP: Baking curved shapes is a little trickier than baking flat shapes, but it's a great skill to know and really adds to the three-dimensional appeal of this project.

1.
Start with a 5" aluminum bowl and a sheet of gingerbread measuring at least 7" x 7". Spray the outside of the bowl with non-stick cooking spray.

2.
Gently flip the sheet of gingerbread over and lay it on top of the bowl. Remove the parchment paper.

3.
Gently smooth the gingerbread over the bowl until it conforms to the shape of the bowl. Trim off the excess at the bottom with a paring knife, leaving about 1" of space between the gingerbread and the lip of the bowl.

4.
4. Bake at 350°F (175°C) on a cookie sheet for about 10 to 13 minutes. Remove the bowl from the oven and immediately trim the bottom edge again. There should be about 1" of space between the bottom of the gingerbread and the lip of the bowl. Let cool completely, then remove the cap.

1. Make a full recipe of gingerbread dough (page 23).

2. Roll out a sheet of gingerbread between two sheets of parchment paper using ⅛" thickness strips (or if you're not using strips, roll the gingerbread as close as possible to ⅛" thick), and then remove top parchment paper. Then cut shapes. You'll need:

   • **5 side pieces**
   • **1 side piece with cutout hole** (use 1½" circle cutter)
   • **3 fin pieces**
   • **1 hexagon base piece** (over-bake this piece to ensure it's very hard when cooled)
   • **1 window frame** (use 2¼" and 1¼" circle cutters)
   • **1 roof cap** (see previous page for baking instructions)
   • **1 spire**

3. Bake according to the guidelines on pages 26–27.

4. Let the pieces cool completely.

5. Repeat steps 2 through 4 until all the pieces are baked.

Bake the ¼" thick gingerbread pieces

(Reference: Working with Gingerbread, pages 18–27)

1. Roll out a sheet of gingerbread between two sheets of parchment paper using ¼" thickness strips (or if you're not using strips, roll the gingerbread as close as possible to ¼" thick),

and then remove top parchment paper. Then cut shapes. You'll need:

   • **4 3" circle pieces**
   • **4 2¼" circle pieces**
   • **1 1½" circle piece**

2. Bake according to the guidelines on pages 26–27.

3. Let the pieces cool completely.

4. Repeat steps 2 through 4 until all the pieces are baked.

Prepare your piping bags

(Reference: Filling a Piping Bag, page 33)

1. Prepare a piping bag with a coupler and a #1 tip and fill with light blue royal icing, reserving about ⅔ of it.

2. Prepare a piping bag with a coupler and a #1 tip and fill with red royal icing, reserving about ½ of it.

Outline and flood the shapes

(Reference: Piping Techniques, pages 35–36; Flooding an Outline, pages 37–38)

1. Pipe outlines around the side piece shapes and fill with light blue royal icing. Make sure to pipe an outline around the window on the piece with the cutout hole.

2. Pipe outlines around the fin shapes with red royal icing.

3. Thin the reserved portions of light blue and red royal icing with small amounts of water (no more than one teaspoon at a time) until you reach the desired flooding consistency.

4. Flood all the outlined shapes with their corresponding colors and let them dry for about 6 hours.

5. Turn the fin shapes over and outline and flood the other side with red royal icing.

6. Attach the window frame on top of the piece with the cutout hole with light blue royal icing.

7. Let all the pieces dry completely overnight.

In the meantime, make the alien's head

(Reference: Rolled Fondant, pages 40–41, and photos on opposite page)

DAY 2

Build the rocket

(Reference: Photos on page 133)

1. Place the hexagon base piece on your work surface.

2. Prepare a piping bag with a coupler and a #4 tip and fill with brown royal icing.

3. Pipe a strip of icing on either side and along the bottom of the front piece of the rocket (the piece with the window).

MAKING THE ALIEN'S HEAD: The alien is my favorite part of this project. Make the head first, and set it aside until you're ready to assemble the rocket.

1.
Tint a 2 oz. piece of fondant green, a ¼-oz. piece blue, a ¼-oz. piece red, and a ¼-oz. piece black (I recommend using pre-tinted red and black fondant).

2.
Shape 1 oz. of the green fondant into an elongated ball and wrap up the rest. With your ball tool, make a depression in the top half of the elongated ball shape for the alien's eye.

3.
Using a small paintbrush, attach a flattened round piece of white fondant for the eyeball with a tiny dab of water. Add a smaller blue one for the iris, an even smaller black one for the pupil, and a tiny white one for the highlight.

4.
Press the bottom of a piping tip into the lower half of the alien's head to create the smile. Using a toothpick, poke holes in either side of the smile.

5.
Add a small rounded piece of red fondant to the top of the alien's head with a tiny dab of water, and flatten slightly.

4. Stand the front piece parallel to one of the sides of the hexagon, about ½" in from the outer edge and attach another side piece to it, aligning it with the adjoining side of the hexagon. The pieces should stand on their own (a).

5. Do the same with a third side piece on the other side. You now have half of the rocket body built.

6. Reinforce the panels by piping thick strips of royal icing along the inside seams and along the bottom where the panels touch the hexagon shape (b).

7. With a bit of brown royal icing, attach a ball of green fondant to the inside of the front window piece, directly underneath the window. This will act as a "shelf" for your alien's head to sit on. Let dry for about an hour (c).

Add the alien and complete the rocket body

(Reference: Photos on page 133)

1. Roll a small rope of green fondant, leaving the end slightly larger. Flatten the end slightly with your fingertip.

2. With a sharp craft knife, cut two lines in the flattened end to form three fingers (d).

3. With your fingertips, separate and round the ends of the fingers.

4. With a little bit of water, attach the arm to the inside of the window, bending the hand slightly so it hooks over the bottom of the windowsill.

5. Attach the head to the fondant "shelf" with a bit of water. The alien now appears to be looking out of the window (e).

6. Continue adding side panels until you've attached all six sides of the rocket body. Every time you add a panel, reinforce it with a strip of icing on the inside. By the time you've added the 5th panel, it will be difficult to reach down to the bottom of the rocket body with your piping bag. That's OK—just pipe the reinforcing strips of icing as far down as you can reach (f).

Add the fondant accents on the sides

(Reference: Rolled Fondant, pages 40–41)

1. Tint a 3-oz. piece of fondant light blue.

2. Make 6 light blue fondant ropes and attach to each corner with a thin strip of light blue royal icing, trimming off the ends at the top and bottom (g).

Build the bottom of the rocket

(Reference: Photos on opposite page)

1. Attach a 3"-circle to your presentation board with a generous amount of brown royal icing.

2. Stack one more 3"-circle and two more 2¼"-circle shapes on top of each other, attaching

each with brown royal icing, and making sure they're level and even (h).

3. Let all the pieces dry completely overnight.

DAY 3

Complete the rocket

(Reference: Photos on opposite page)

1. Attach the body of the rocket to the top of the circles. It's important that the body of the rocket dries straight and level; to ensure this, hold the rocket in place for about 5 minutes until the icing sets (i).

2. Attach the fin pieces to the rocket body with light blue royal icing. Let set for a few minutes.

3. Tint a 3-oz. piece of rolled fondant red (or to make it easier, use pre-tinted red fondant).

4. Roll three red fondant ropes and attach to the outside of the fins with light blue royal icing, trimming off the ends at the bottom (j).

5. With a piping bag fitted with a #4 tip and brown royal icing, pipe a large dot of royal icing on each top corner of the rocket body and set the rounded cap down on it, making sure that it sits level. You can use a generous amount of

icing for this step, as it will be completely hidden.

6. Add two 3"-circles, two 2¼"-circles, and one 1½"-circle cookies to the top of the cap, sandwiching each one together with brown royal icing (k).

7. With a large dot of brown royal icing, attach the spire to the top (you may have to hold it in place for a few minutes as it sets).

8. Roll out a red fondant rope and attach around the base of the circle cookies, trimming off the ends where it meets.

9. Attach mini candy-coated chocolate "lights" around the top of the cap, the base of the spire, and the bottom hexagon shape (l).

10. Cut large red gumdrops in half and attach to the top of each fin with a bit of light blue royal icing.

a.

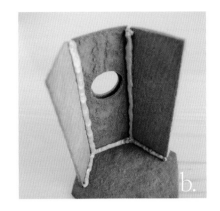

b.

c.

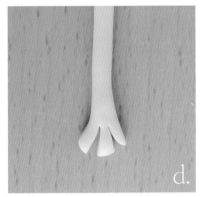

d.

e.

f.

g.

h.

i.

j.

k.

l.

CHESS SET

Chess enthusiasts will love this all-edible chess set—when you take your opponent's piece, you can eat it too! Made with both chocolate and regular gingerbread, the squares are fitted together before they're baked to create one single checkered grid. The challenge with this project lies mostly in the baking—there are lots of individual little pieces, but the end result is really impressive! Checkmate!

Yield: 1 chess set
Difficulty Level: 4
Finished Size: About 11" x 11"

RECIPES

- ½ royal icing recipe *(page 31)*
- 1 gingerbread recipe *(page 23)*
- 1 chocolate gingerbread recipe *(page 23)*

TOOLS

- Pencil and eraser
- Ruler
- Cutting mat
- Craft knife
- Scissors
- Basic baking equipment (stand mixer or sturdy hand mixer, bowls, measuring cups and spoons, sieve, rubber spatula)
- Toothpick

- Small bowl
- Small spoon
- Airtight plastic containers for storing icing colors
- Rolling pin (large)
- ⅛" thickness strips
- Paring knife
- Cookie sheet
- Cooling rack
- One piping bag and coupler set
- One #4 piping tip
- One #2 piping tip

MATERIALS

- Foam core (for presentation board)
- Ribbon to trim presentation board

- Brown food coloring gel
- Parchment paper
- About 8 oz. rolled fondant tinted brown (I recommend pre-tinted fondant)

CUTTERS

- 1" circle cutter
- ⅝" circle cutter
- Miniature gingerbread man
- Miniature gingerbread woman

- Making a presentation board *(page 13)*
- Making royal icing *(page 31)*
- Coloring royal icing *(page 32)*
- Storing royal icing *(page 32)*
- Preparing the dough *(page 22)*
- Rolling and cutting the dough *(pages 24–25)*
- Baking basics *(pages 26–27)*
- Filling a piping bag *(page 33)*
- Piping techniques *(pages 35–36)*
- Coloring, rolling, and shaping rolled fondant *(pages 40–41)*

METHOD

DAY 1

Prepare your presentation board

(Reference: Presentation Boards, page 13)

I recommend that the presentation board for this project be at least 13" x 13" square.

Make royal icing

(Reference: Royal Icing, pages 30–33)

1. Make a half recipe of royal icing *(page 31)*. Divide roughly in half and tint one half brown. Leave the other half white; keep it for another project.

2. Cover each color tightly with plastic wrap or transfer to airtight containers and set aside.

Bake the chess board

(Reference: Working with Gingerbread, pages 18–27)

1. Make a full recipe of regular gingerbread dough and a full recipe of chocolate gingerbread dough *(page 23)*.

2. Roll out a sheet of gingerbread between two sheets of parchment paper using ⅛"thickness strips (or if you're not using strips, roll the gingerbread as close as possible to ⅛" thick), and then remove top parchment paper. Then cut 32 squares each measuring 1¼" square.

3. Repeat step 2 using chocolate gingerbread.

4. Place both sheets of gingerbread in the freezer for about 20 minutes.

5. With the tip of a paring knife, transfer the frozen squares one by one, alternating colors, to a new sheet of parchment so that they form a grid—each side of the grid should have 8 squares *(see photos and additional instructions on the next page)*.

6. Bake according to the guidelines on pages 26–27.

7. Let the pieces cool completely.

Bake the individual chess pieces

(Reference: Working with Gingerbread, pages 18–27)

1. Roll out a sheet of gingerbread between two sheets of parch-ment paper using ⅛" thickness strips (or if you're not using strips, roll the gingerbread as close as possible to ⅛" thick), and then remove top parchment paper. Then cut shapes. You'll need:

    - **18 1" circles**
    - **27 ⅝" circles**
    - **5 ⅝" circles, cut in half and separated before baking**
    - **2 horsehead shapes (to make these, cut 2 1" circles, then use the same cutter to trim two edges off—see photo below)**
    - **9 small gingerbread balls (to make these, cut out ⅝" circles and roll each circle into a ball—see photo below)**
    - **3 miniature gingerbread men**
    - **1 miniature gingerbread lady**

2. Bake according to the guidelines on pages 26–27.

3. Let the pieces cool completely.

4. Repeat steps 1 through 3 using chocolate gingerbread.

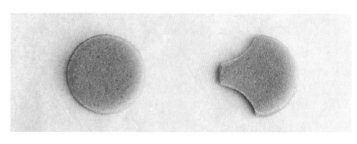

BAKING THE CHESS BOARD: Be sure to measure and cut the individual squares as accurately as possible to ensure that they'll line up evenly.

1.
Measure, cut, and freeze 32 squares of each chocolate and regular gingerbread for 20 minutes. Lift each square with the tip of a paring knife and transfer to another baking sheet, alternating each color.

2.
You should end up with a square grid—each side should have 8 squares. Make sure the sides are evenly aligned and bake as directed.

ASSEMBLING THE PIECES: The knight, bishop, king, and queen pieces require two half circles to be placed on either side of the part of the piece that's standing upright. The knight is shown below, but the technique is the same for all the pieces.

1.
Start with the base piece, the two half circles, and the piece that will stand upright.

2.
With brown royal icing and a #2 tip, pipe a large dot in the middle of the base piece and two dots on either side of it.

3.
Place the upright piece on the middle dot of royal icing and a half circle on each side on top of the outer dots. Hold in place for a minute if necessary.

Prepare your piping bags

(Reference: Filling a Piping Bag, page 33)

1. Prepare a piping bag with a coupler and a #4 tip and fill with brown royal icing.

Assemble the pieces

(Reference: Photos below and on opposite page)

1. Using the below photo for reference, assemble the chess pieces. Start from the bottom and add the pieces as you move up, attaching with a dot of brown royal icing and letting each of the larger pieces dry for a few minutes between additions. The knight, bishop, king, and queen are supported by a half-circle on each side; for a detailed explanation on how the half-circle works to support the pieces, *(see assembly instructions and photos on opposite page)*. For each color, you should end up with 8 pawns, 2 rooks, 2 knights, 2 bishops, 1 king, and 1 queen.

2. Let all pieces dry for about 2 hours before moving them.

Finish the board

(Reference: Rolled Fondant, pages 40–41)

1. Attach the chess board to your presentation board with a generous amount of brown royal icing.

2. Tint 8 oz. of rolled fondant dark brown (or to make it easier, use pre-tinted chocolate fondant).

3. Roll thick ropes and attach them to the edges of the chess board with a strip of royal icing, trimming at each end with a craft knife to angle the corners.

4. Place the chess pieces on the board.

5. Let all the pieces dry completely overnight.

ROBOT

This guy might just be too cute to eat! Gingerbread and candy perfectly re-create the colorful, chunky, and adorably awkward look of vintage robots of the 1950s. Except for his mouth, there's no decorative piping involved with this project, but building him requires some time and patience to ensure he's stable—he should be made over a few days.

Yield: 1 robot
Difficulty Level: 4
Finished Size: About 12" high

RECIPES

- 1 royal icing recipe *(page 31)*
- 1 gingerbread recipe *(page 23)*

TOOLS

- Scissors
- Pencil and eraser
- Ruler
- Cutting mat
- Craft knife
- Glue gun
- Basic baking equipment (stand mixer or sturdy hand mixer, bowls, measuring cups and spoons, sieve, rubber spatula)
- Toothpicks
- Small bowls
- Small spoons
- Airtight plastic containers for storing icing colors

- Rolling pin (large)
- ⅛" thickness strips
- ¼" thickness strips
- Paring knife
- Cookie sheet
- Cooling rack
- Two piping bags and sets of couplers
- One #1 piping tip
- One #4 piping tip

MATERIALS

- Foam core or thick cardboard (for templates)
- Foam core (for presentation board)
- Ribbon to trim presentation board
- Green and brown food coloring gel
- Parchment paper

- Assorted colors of ring candies
- Red-and-white-striped mints
- Small round green gumdrops
- Mini candy-coated chocolates in assorted colors
- One large green gumdrop

CUTTERS

- 1" circle cutter
- 1½" circle cutter
- ⅝" circle cutter (or the back of a small piping tip)

TEMPLATES

The templates for this project can be found on pages 168–171.

TECHNIQUES USED

- Making a template *(page 11)*
- Making a presentation board *(page 13)*
- Making royal icing *(page 31)*
- Coloring royal icing *(page 32)*

- Storing royal icing *(page 32)*
- Preparing the dough *(page 22)*
- Rolling and cutting the dough *(pages 24–25)*
- Baking basics *(pages 26–27)*

- Filling a piping bag *(page 33)*
- Piping techniques *(pages 35–36)*
- Flooding an outline *(pages 37–38)*
- Construction basics *(pages 42–45)*

METHOD

DAY 1

Prepare your templates

(Reference: Making a Template, page 11)

You can use either foam core or thick cardboard to make most of the templates for this project. For the smaller pieces I recommend using a thinner material, such as heavy cardboard or thick paper. The templates can be found on pages 168–171.

Prepare your presentation board

(Reference: Presentation Boards, page 13)

I recommend that the presentation board for this project be at least 6½" x 6½" square or 8" round.

Make royal icing

(Reference: Royal Icing, pages 30–33)

1. Make a full recipe of royal icing *(page 31)*.

2. Divide it roughly in half; tint one half light green and the other half brown.

3. Cover each color tightly with plastic wrap or transfer to airtight containers and set aside.

Bake the ⅛" thick gingerbread pieces

(Reference: Working with Gingerbread, pages 18–27)

Note: For this project, you'll cut some shapes from ⅛" thick dough and some from ¼" thick dough.

1. Make a full recipe of gingerbread dough *(page 23)*.

2. Roll out a sheet of gingerbread between two sheets of parchment paper using ⅛" thickness strips (or if you're not using strips, roll the gingerbread as close as possible to ⅛" thick), and then remove top parchment paper. Then cut shapes. You'll need:

   • **1 front head piece**
   • **1 back head piece**
   • **2 side head pieces**
   • **1 top head piece**
   • **1 bottom head piece**
   • **1 front body piece**
   • **1 back body piece**
   • **2 side body pieces**
   • **1 top body piece**
   • **1 body support piece**
   • **4 side leg pieces**
   • **4 foot pieces**
   • **7 1" circles**
   • **4 1½" circles**
   • **1 square front accent piece**
   • **1 rectangular front accent piece**

3. Bake according to the guidelines on pages 26–27.

4. Let the pieces cool completely.

5. Repeat steps 2 through 4 until all the pieces are baked.

Bake the ¼" thick gingerbread pieces

(Reference: Working with Gingerbread, pages 18–27)

1. Roll out a sheet of gingerbread between two sheets of parchment paper using ¼" thickness strips (or if you're not using strips, roll the gingerbread as close as possible to ¼" thick), and then remove top parchment paper. Then cut shapes. You'll need:

   • **4 inside leg pieces**
   • **4 front leg pieces**
   • **4 back leg pieces**
   • **1 bottom body base piece (Important: overbake this piece until it's dark brown. It needs to be extra hard to provide added support.)**
   • **4 arm pieces**
   • **2 hand pieces (to cut hands, cut out a 1½" circle, then a ⅝" circle inside it. Cut two parallel lines from the inside circle to the outside so that when the excess is removed, the hand resembles a C shape.)**

TRY THIS!

The robot's head makes a perfect candy box—it's even got its own little handle. Just omit the step of attaching the top piece of the head with royal icing, and when the robot's finished, fill his head with delicious candy!

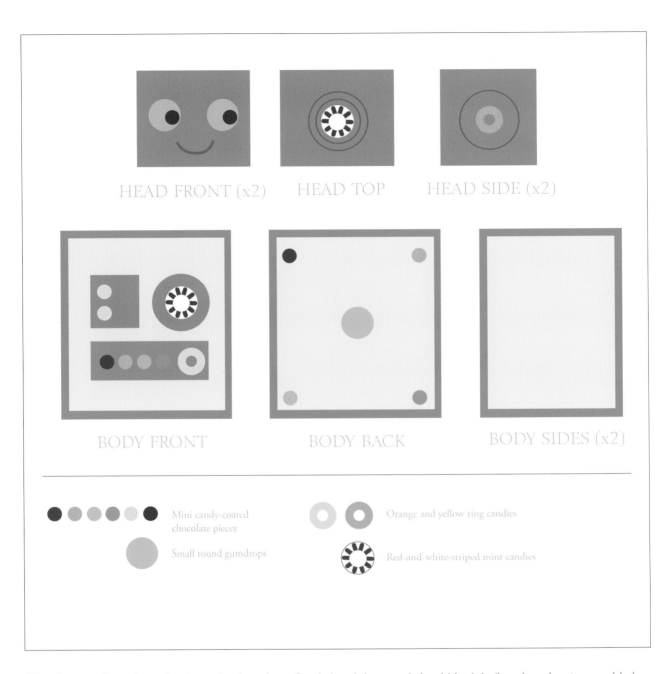

HEAD FRONT (x2)   HEAD TOP   HEAD SIDE (x2)

BODY FRONT   BODY BACK   BODY SIDES (x2)

Mini candy-coated chocolate pieces

Small round gumdrops

Orange and yellow ring candies

Red-and-white-striped mint candies

This diagram shows how the pieces that have been flooded and decorated should look before the robot is assembled. Use it as a guide for attaching candies and accent pieces.

2. Bake according to the guidelines on pages 26–27.

3. Let the pieces cool completely.

4. Repeat steps 1 through 3 until all the pieces are baked.

Prepare your piping bags

(Reference: Filling a Piping Bag, page 33)

1. Prepare a piping bag with a coupler and a #1 tip and fill with light green royal icing, reserving about ½ of it.

2. Prepare a piping bag with a coupler and a #4 tip and fill with brown royal icing.

Outline and flood the shapes

(Reference: Piping Techniques, pages 35–36; Flooding an Outline, pages 37–38)

1. Pipe outlines around the front, back, side, and top body pieces with light green royal icing.

2. Thin the reserved portion of light green royal icing with small amounts of water (no more than one teaspoon at a time) until you reach the desired flooding consistency.

3. Flood all the outlined shapes with the thinned light green royal icing.

4. Let the pieces dry for about 2 hours.

Decorate the shapes

(Reference: Piping Techniques, pages 35–36)

1. Using the illustrations as a guide, add the accent pieces and candies to the front body, face, and the sides and top of the head, using brown royal icing and a #4 tip.

2. Switch the tip to a #1 and pipe a smile on the robot's face.

Assemble the arms, legs, and feet

(Reference: Photos on page 147)

1. Using the photos and illustrations as reference, assemble the arms, legs, and feet (a through c).

2. Attach the feet to the middle of the presentation board with a large dot of brown royal icing (d).

3. Let everything dry completely overnight.

DAY 2

Assemble the robot's body and head

(Reference: Photos on page 147)

1. Place the overbaked bottom body piece on your work surface.

2. With a piping bag fitted with a #4 tip, pipe brown royal icing along the back edge of the front piece and stand up on the

bottom piece, attaching the corresponding side piece to it. You should be able to let it stand on its own right away (e).

3. Pipe thick lines of royal icing along all the inside seams.

4. Pipe a strip of royal icing along the front edge of the second side piece and attach it. Reinforce the inner seams (f).

5. Pipe strips of royal icing along each edge of the back piece and attach it. Reinforce the inner seams, reaching down as far as you can with your piping bag.

6. Pipe a strip around the top edges of the assembled body and attach the top piece to it.

7. Following the same general steps as the body, assemble the robot's head (g).

8. Let the body and head dry for about 6 hours.

Attach the arms

(Reference: Photos on opposite page)

1. Lay the robot's body gently on its back.

2. Pipe strips of brown royal icing along the bottom surface of the robot's arms and press the arms onto the body, holding gently in place for a few minutes.

Attach the legs to the feet

(Reference: Photos on opposite page)

1. Pipe a generous amount of royal icing on the bottom of each leg and attach to the feet, making sure they sit level (h).

2. Attach the body support piece to the top of the legs with a generous amount of royal icing, again making sure it's level (i).

3. Let all the pieces dry completely overnight.

DAY 3

Do the final assembly

(Reference: Photos on opposite page)

1. Pipe a generous amount of brown royal icing on the base support piece.

2. Place the robot's body gently on top of the base support piece, holding in place for a minute or two to ensure it is level (j).

3. Pipe a generous amount of royal icing on the bottom of the robot's head and place on top of the body.

4. Cut a large green gumdrop in half and attach to the top of the robot's arms with the cut side facing inward (k).

5. Place a red-and-white-striped mint candy in the robot's hand (l). If necessary, secure it with a bit of royal icing. Be careful during this step—the robot's arms are definitely his most fragile parts!

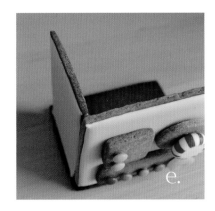

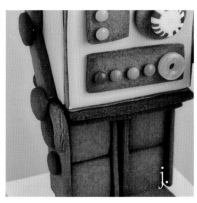

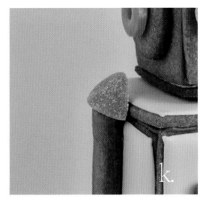

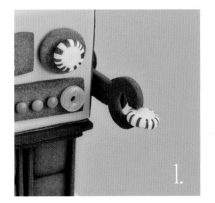

SHOWHOME

This project combines both chocolate and regular gingerbread with elaborate piping and charming details to create a stunning effect. The two trees inside the house that can be seen through the open windows are added touches that give the house even more charm. Display this gorgeous home in a prominent place over the holidays—it's sure to be a showstopper!

Yield: 1 house
Difficulty Level: 4
Finished Size: About 10½" high

WHAT YOU'LL NEED

RECIPES

- 1 royal icing recipe *(page 31)*
- 1 gingerbread recipe *(page 23)*
- 1 chocolate gingerbread recipe *(page 23)*

TOOLS

- Scissors
- Pencil and eraser
- Ruler
- Cutting mat
- Craft knife
- Glue gun
- Basic baking equipment (stand mixer or sturdy hand mixer, bowls, measuring cups and spoons, sieve, rubber spatula)
- Toothpicks
- Small bowls
- Small spoons
- Airtight plastic containers for storing icing colors
- Rolling pin (large)
- ⅛" thickness strips
- ¼" thickness strips
- Paring knife
- Cookie sheet
- Cooling rack
- Five piping bags and sets of couplers
- Five #1 piping tips
- One #4 piping tip
- Serrated-edge knife
- One #67 leaf piping tip
- One #10 piping tip

MATERIALS

- Foam core or thick cardboard (for templates)
- Foam core (for presentation board)
- Ribbon to trim presentation board
- Green, blue, red, and brown food coloring gel
- Parchment paper
- 8 sugar cones

CUTTERS

- 1½" circle cutter (window top)
- 2¼" circle cutter (door top)

TEMPLATES

The templates for this project can be found on pages 172–180.

TECHNIQUES USED

- Making a template *(page 11)*
- Making a presentation board *(page 13)*
- Making royal icing *(page 31)*
- Coloring royal icing *(page 32)*
- Storing royal icing *(page 32)*
- Preparing the dough *(page 22)*
- Rolling and cutting the dough *(pages 24–25)*
- Baking basics *(pages 26–27)*
- Filling a piping bag *(page 33)*
- Piping techniques *(pages 35–36)*
- Flooding an outline *(pages 37–38)*
- Construction basics *(pages 42–45)*

METHOD

DAY 1

Prepare your templates

(Reference: Making a Template, page 11)

You can use either foam core or thick cardboard to make most of the templates for this project. For the smaller pieces I recommend using a thinner material, such as heavy cardboard or thick paper. The templates can be found on pages 172–180.

Prepare your presentation board

(Reference: Presentation Boards, page 13)

I recommend that the presentation board for this project be at least 10" x 13". A rectangular board works best for this house.

Make royal icing

(Reference: Royal Icing, pages 30–33)

1. Make a full recipe of royal icing *(page 31)*.

2. Divide it roughly into three portions; tint one portion green.

3. Divide the next portion in half; tint one half blue and the other half red.

4. Divide the last portion in half; tint one half brown and leave the other half white.

5. Cover each color tightly with plastic wrap or transfer to airtight containers and set aside.

Bake the ⅛" thick regular gingerbread pieces

(Reference: Working with Gingerbread, pages 18–27)

Note: For this project, you'll cut some shapes from ⅛" thick dough and some from ¼" thick dough.

1. Make a full recipe of regular gingerbread dough *(page 23)*.

2. Roll out a sheet of gingerbread between two sheets of parchment paper using ⅛" thickness strips (or if you're not using strips, roll the gingerbread as close as possible to ⅛" thick), and then remove top parchment paper. Then cut shapes. You'll need:

- **1 front piece A with window cutouts***
- **1 front piece B with door cutout**
- **1 back piece**
- **2 side pieces with window cutouts**
- **1 back door piece**
- **1 floor piece**
- **3 floor support pieces**
- **1 doorstop piece**

*See page 121 for tips on cutting rectangular windows.

3. Bake according to the guidelines on pages 26–27.

4. Let the pieces cool completely.

5. Repeat steps 2 through 4 until all the pieces are baked.

Bake the ¼" thick regular gingerbread pieces

(Reference: Working with Gingerbread, pages 18–27)

1. Roll out a sheet of gingerbread between two sheets of parchment paper using ¼" thickness strips (or if you're not using strips, roll the gingerbread as close as possible to ¼" thick), and then remove top parchment paper. Then cut shapes. You'll need:

- **1 large front step piece**
- **1 medium front step piece**
- **1 small front step piece**

2. Bake according to the guidelines on pages 26–27.

3. Let the pieces cool completely.

4. Repeat steps 1 through 3 until all the pieces are baked.

Bake the chocolate gingerbread pieces

(Reference: Working with Gingerbread, pages 18–27)

1. Make a full recipe of chocolate gingerbread dough *(page 23)*.

2. Roll out a sheet of gingerbread between two sheets of parchment paper using ⅛" thickness strips (or if you're not using strips, roll the gingerbread as close as possible to ⅛" thick),

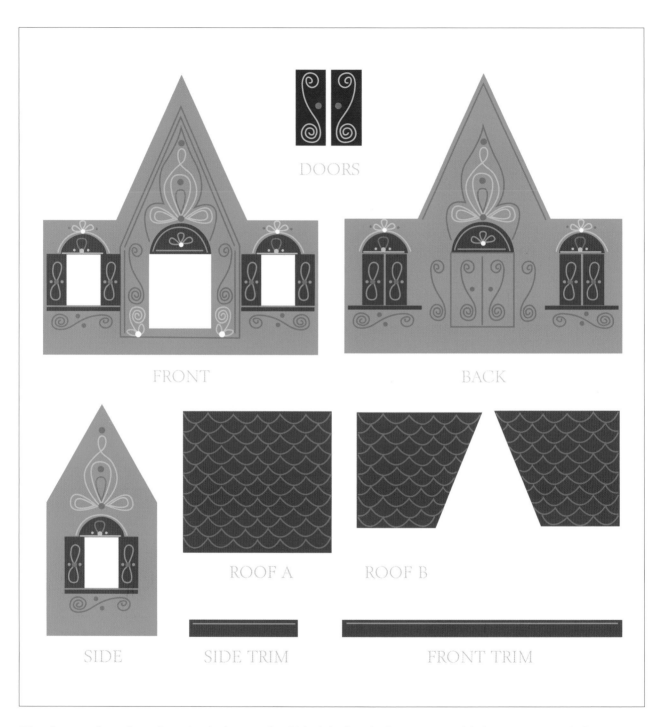

DOORS

FRONT

BACK

ROOF A

ROOF B

SIDE

SIDE TRIM

FRONT TRIM

This diagram shows how the individual pieces should look before the house is assembled. Use it as a guide for piping lines and dots, and attaching the window tops and shutters.

and then remove top parchment paper. Then cut shapes. You'll need:

- **2 roof A pieces**
- **4 roof B pieces (cut one set with the templates face up, then flip the templates over and cut two mirror image pieces for a total of four roof pieces)**
- **2 front door pieces (overbake these pieces to a very dark brown, almost black shade)**
- **12 window shutters**
- **6 window top pieces (2 1½" circles, cut in half and separated)**
- **6 window bottom pieces**
- **2 door top pieces (2 2¼" circles, cut in half and separated)**
- **2 long trim pieces**
- **2 short trim pieces**

3. Bake according to the guidelines on pages 26–27.

4. Let the pieces cool completely.

5. Repeat steps 2 through 4 until all the pieces are baked.

Prepare your piping bags

(Reference: Filling a Piping Bag, page 33)

1. Prepare four piping bags with couplers and #1 tips.

2. Fill one piping bag with white royal icing, one with green royal icing, one with red royal icing, and one with blue royal icing.

3. Prepare one piping bag with a coupler and a #4 tip and fill with brown royal icing.

Assemble the front piece

1. Place the front trim piece along the bottom of the front piece but do NOT attach. You'll be using this as a guide only and will attach it later.

2. Attach front piece B to front piece A using a generous amount of brown royal icing in between the pieces. Remove the front trim piece.

3. Attach the shutters and the top and bottom window pieces to the front piece.

4. Attach the door top piece.

Assemble the side pieces

1. Attach the shutters and the

MAKING THE TREES: All you need is a piping bag, a leaf tip, and sugar cones to make these trees.

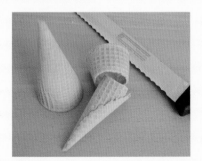

1.
With a serrated-edge knife, cut the bottoms on a few sugar cones so they're varied in height, making sure the bottoms are level.

2.
2. Switch the tip on your green piping bag to a #67 tip. Starting at the bottom, pipe leaves around the cone, twirling it as you go and slowly working upward.

3.
3. When you reach the top, pipe a single leaf pointing upward. Let the cones dry overnight.

top and bottom window pieces to the side pieces.

Assemble the back pieces

1. Place the back trim piece along the bottom of the back piece but do NOT attach. You'll be using this as a guide only and will attach it later.

2. Attach the back door piece with a generous amount of royal icing.

3. Attach the shutters, the bottom and top window pieces, and the top door piece.

Decorate the shapes

(Reference: Piping Techniques, pages 35–36)

1. Switch the tip on your brown piping bag to a #1 tip.

2. Using the illustrations and photos as a guide, pipe lines and dots on the front, back, and side pieces with red, blue, brown, green, and white royal icing.

3. Pipe scalloped lines on the roof pieces with brown royal icing to resemble shingles.

4. Let all the pieces dry completely overnight.

In the meantime, make the trees

(Reference: Instructions and photos on previous page)

DAY 2

Assemble the house

(Reference: The Basics of Construction, pages 42–45; Piping Techniques, pages 35–36)

1. With a piping bag fitted with a #4 tip and filled with brown royal icing, assemble the floor directly on your presentation board (a through c). Position the floor so that there is more space at the front of the presentation board than at the back (to accommodate the stairs).

2. Pipe a strip of brown royal icing along the back of the front piece where it meets the floor piece and attach it (d).

3. Pipe a strip of royal icing along the back of a side piece where it meets the floor piece, as well as along the edge where it will join the front piece, and attach (e).

4. Attach the other side piece and the back piece in a similar manner until all the walls are standing.

5. Pipe thick reinforcing strips of royal icing along the inner wall seams. Let the pieces dry for about 6 hours.

6. Attach one of the trees on each side of the floor on the inside so that they sit right in front of each of the front windows (f).

7. Pipe strips of icing on the top edges of the house where the Roof A pieces will be attached (g).

8. Immediately place the Roof A pieces on the house and hold together gently but firmly, for about 5 minutes, until the icing has set enough so that the pieces will stay on their own. Pipe a strip of icing along the roof seam for extra reinforcement.

9. Pipe strips of icing on the top edges of the house where the Roof B pieces will be attached (h).

10. Immediately place the Roof B pieces on the house and hold together gently but firmly, for about 5 minutes, until the icing has set enough so that the pieces will stay on their own. Pipe a strip of icing along the roof seam for extra reinforcement. Do the same for the other side of the roof.

11. Add the trim pieces to the front, back, and sides of the house (i).

12. Attach the stairs one by one to the front of the house with a large dot of royal icing, starting with the bottom stair and working up to the top stair (j). Attach the doorstop piece to cover the gap between the stairs and floor. Attach the door pieces.

13. With a piping bag fitted with a #10 tip and filled with white royal icing, pipe snow around the base of the house, around the edges and seams of the roof, and on the windowsills (k).

14. Place the remaining trees around the house and pipe white royal icing around them to attach them to the presentation board (l).

 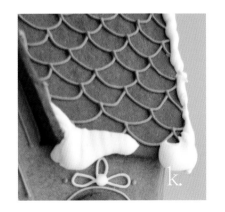 

TEMPLATES

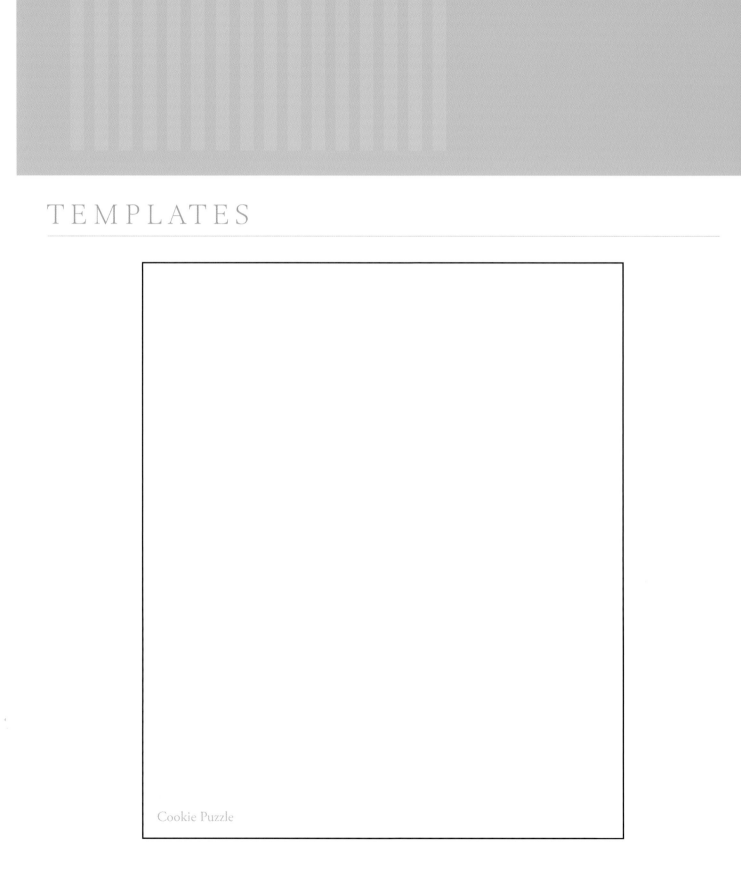

Cookie Puzzle

Ornament Front
and Back

Ornament
Side

Ornament
Roof

Toy Box Front and Back

Toy Box Side

Toy Box Base and Lid

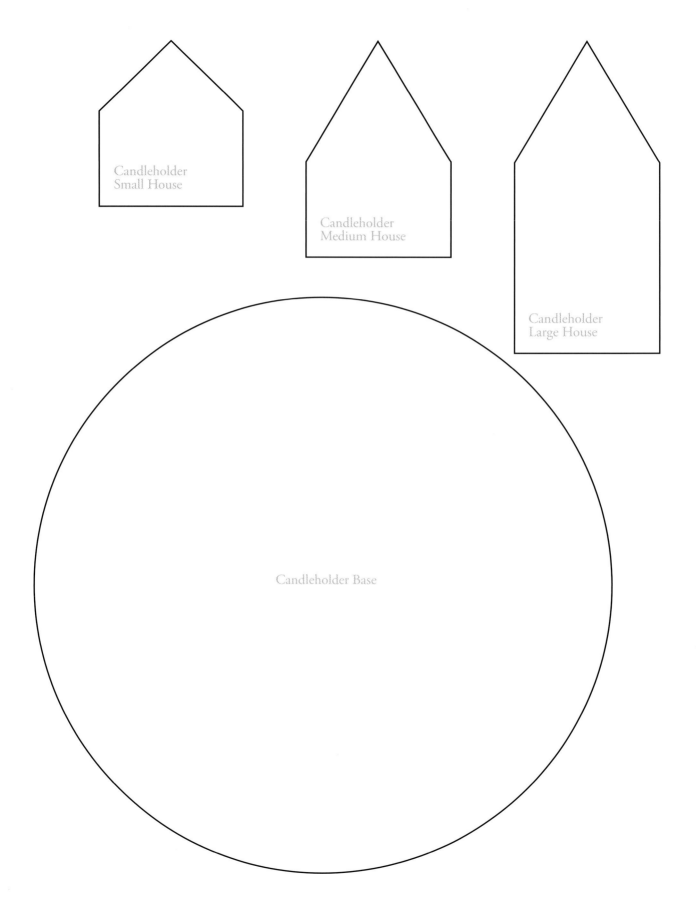

Candleholder
Small House

Candleholder
Medium House

Candleholder
Large House

Candleholder Base

Candy-Filled House Front
and Back

Candy-Filled House Roof

Candy-Filled House Side

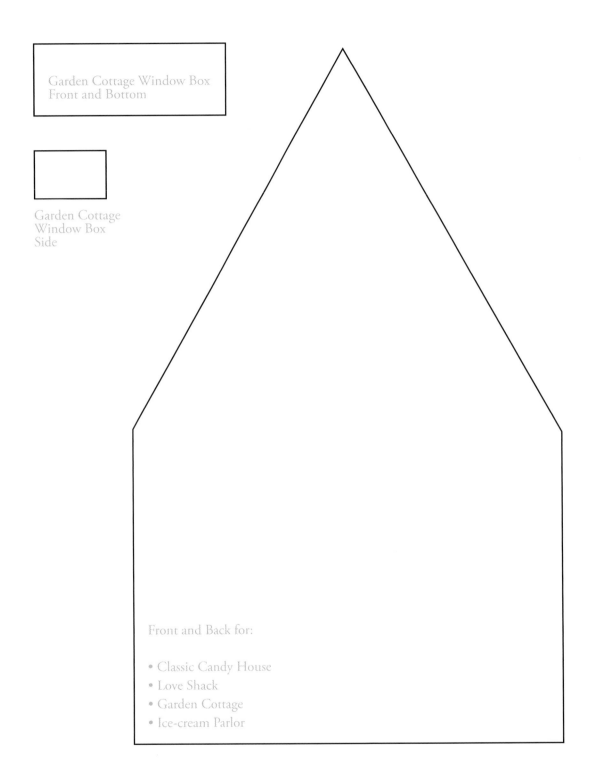

Garden Cottage Window Box
Front and Bottom

Garden Cottage
Window Box
Side

Front and Back for:

• Classic Candy House
• Love Shack
• Garden Cottage
• Ice-cream Parlor

Roof for:

• Classic Candy House
• Love Shack
• Garden Cottage
• Ice-cream Parlor
• Haunted House

Side for:

• Classic Candy House
• Love Shack
• Garden Cottage
• Ice-cream Parlor

Birdhouse Front and Back

Birdhouse Front Accent Piece

Birdhouse Side Accent Piece

Birdhouse Side and Roof

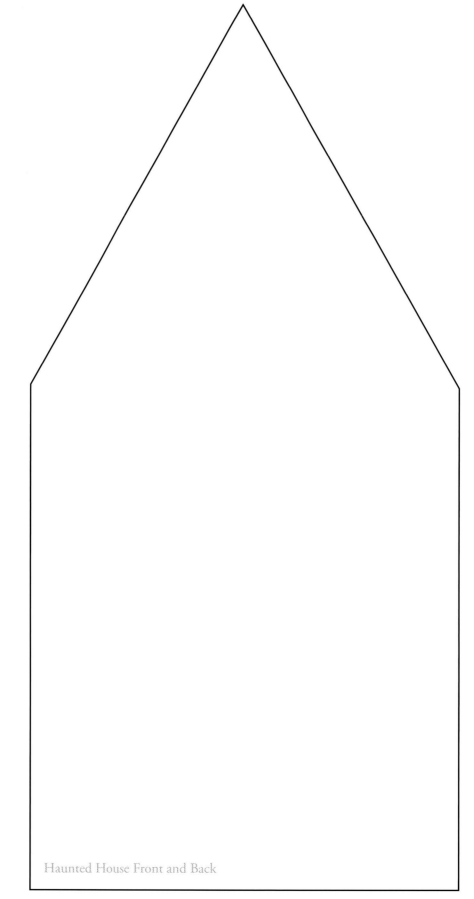

Haunted House Front and Back

Haunted House Inner
Door

Haunted House
Window Cutout

Haunted House
Inner Window

Haunted
House
Shutter

Haunted House Side

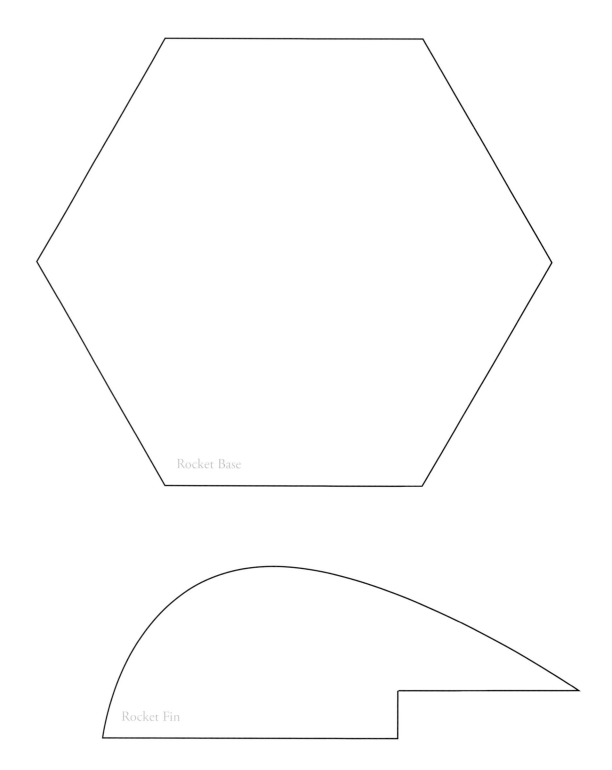

Rocket Base

Rocket Fin

Rocket Side

Rocket Spire

Robot Body Top and Bottom

Robot Body Side

Robot Body Front and Back

Robot Head Front and Back

Front Rectangular Accent

Robot Leg Side

Robot Arm

Robot Body Support Piece

Robot Head Side

Robot Head Top and Bottom

Robot Leg
Front and Back

Robot Inside Leg

Robot Foot

Front Square
Accent

Showhome Front A (**PHOTOCOPY AT 125%**)

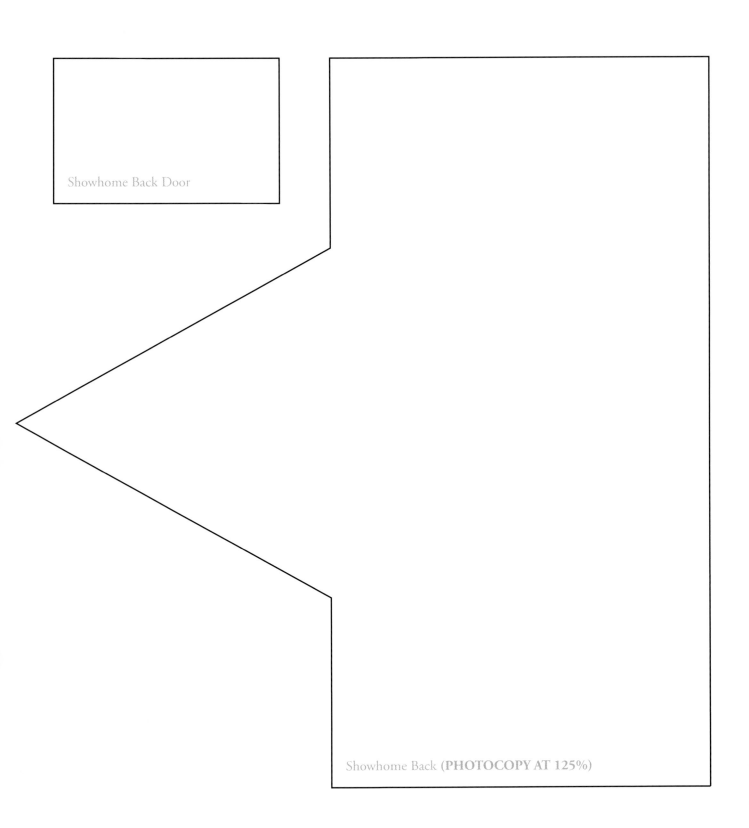

Showhome Back Door

Showhome Back (**PHOTOCOPY AT 125%**)

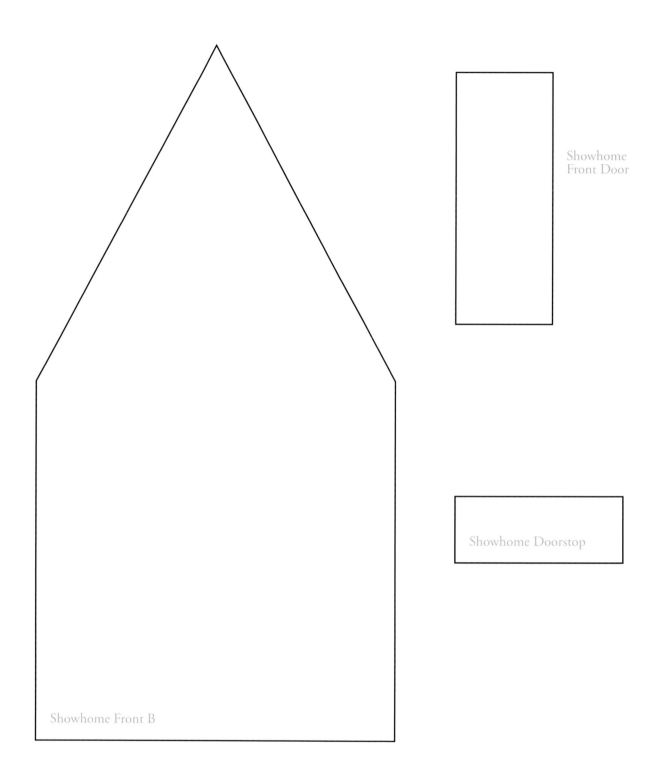

Showhome Front Door

Showhome Doorstop

Showhome Front B

Showhome
Window Shutter

Showhome
Window Cutout

Showhome Bottom Window

Showhome Front Door
Cutout for Front B

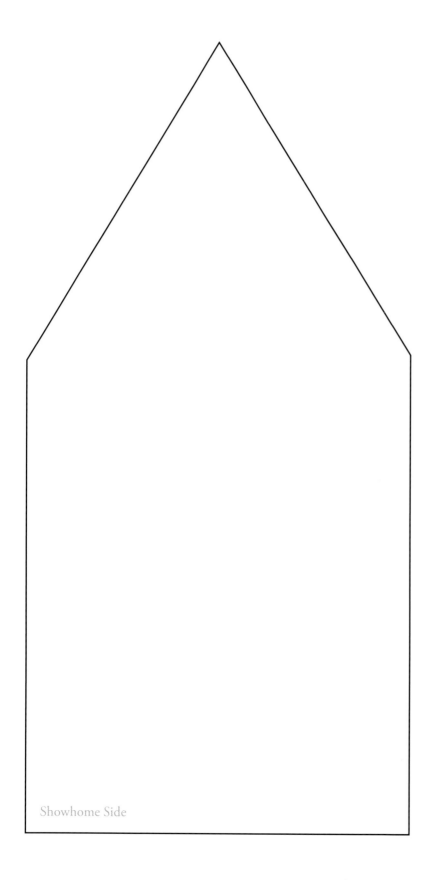

Showhome Side

Showhome Long
Trim **(PHOTOCOPY AT 110%)**

Showhome
Small Front Step

Showhome
Medium Front Step

Showhome
Short
Trim

Showhome
Large Front Step

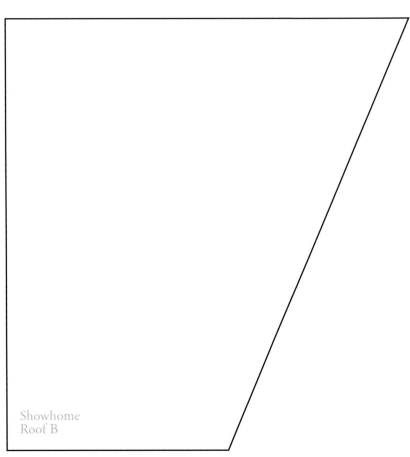

Showhome
Roof B

Showhome
Roof A

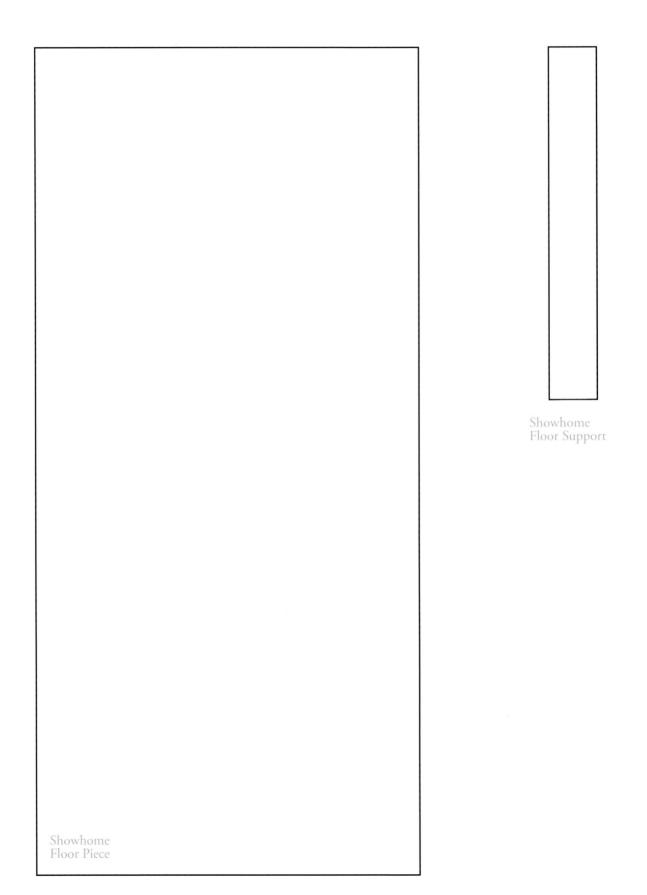

Showhome
Floor Piece

Showhome
Floor Support

MEASUREMENT CONVERSIONS

Frequently used measurements in this book:

INCHES	CENTIMETERS
¹⁄₁₆	0.16
⅛	0.32
³⁄₁₆	0.48
¼	0.64
⅓	0.85
½	1.27
⅝	1.59
¾	1.91
1	2.54
1¼	3.18
1½	3.81
2	5.08
2¼	5.72
2½	6.35
3	7.62
3½	8.89
3¾	9.53
4	10.16
4½	11.43
5	12.7
6	15.24
6½	16.51
7	17.78
7½	19.05
8	20.32
9	22.86
10	25.4
10½	26.67
11	27.94
12	30.48
13	33.02

SOURCES

Although you can find the tools and materials used in this book from various sources, here are some of my recommended sources.

Bulk Barn Foods Limited

Baking and cake decorating supplies, and bulk candy

bulkbarn.ca

Stores located across Canada

Canadian Tire Stores

Baking and cake decorating supplies

canadiantire.ca

Stores located across Canada

Golda's Kitchen

Bake and cake decorating supplies

goldaskitchen.com

Icing Inspirations

Cake supply shop

icinginspirations.com

14 Hoffman Street, Unit 4

Kitchener, ON

N2M 3M4

Michaels Arts and Crafts Stores

Baking and cake decorating supplies

michaels.com

Stores located across Canada and the United States

Satin Ice

Premium quality rolled fondant

satinice.com

Wilton Industries

Baking and cake decorating supplies

wilton.com

ACKNOWLEDGMENTS

Writing this book has been the single most enjoyable and rewarding experience of my career to date, and I am grateful to many people for helping to make it happen:

A huge thanks goes to Robert Lecker, my agent, who from the very beginning was enthusiastic about the idea of a book about gingerbread and whose continuous support inspired me to do my best work possible. Thank you so much Robert.

Thank you to Mara Conlon and the editing team at Peter Pauper Press, for making the editing process easy and enjoyable. Your enthusiasm, ideas, and suggestions were invaluable and always appreciated.

To Sonia Mendes, for your generous help in editing my proposal, and Ian Mendes, for your patience in answering my many questions, and to both of you for your unending support, thank you.

To Jen McGill, thank you for your design advice and valuable InDesign tips whenever I needed them.

Thank you to Chef Tony Bond, whose gingerbread recipe is by far the best I've ever used.

My niece and nephew, Layla and Mason Cheikh, enthusiastically posed for photos for this book, and proved themselves well deserving of the gingerbread and candy payment they received in return. Thank you, sweeties.

Many thanks go to all the family members, friends, clients, colleagues, and students who encouraged and supported me throughout the entire process of writing this book.

I cannot thank my two wonderful daughters, Annabelle and Sasha, enough for all the love, encouragement, and enthusiasm they have given me, during the process of writing this book and in every other way as well. Thank you my sweethearts for all your help, in so many ways, from posing for photos, to taste testing, making suggestions, and doing your best to give me space to work. I love you so much.

Finally, my love and biggest thanks goes to my husband, Tyler Bailey. The bottom line is, without your support in way too many ways to list here, this book would not have been possible.